D0392335

April 21, 2011

Hauoli La Hanau!

(Happy Birthday in Hawaiian...)

We heard that this one was one
of the best books about wine.
And it's short - perfect for you.

We Love you!

Britt, Dave, Gemma...

p.s. this one's on my
readinglist too!
I'm curious to know
what you think!

READING BETWEEN THE WINES

Terry Theise

University of California Press   Berkeley   Los Angeles   London

University of California Press, one of the most distin-
guished university presses in the United States, enriches
lives around the world by advancing scholarship in the
humanities, social sciences, and natural sciences. Its activi-
ties are supported by the UC Press Foundation and by
philanthropic contributions from individuals and institu-
tions. For more information, visit www.ucpress.edu.

University of California Press
Berkeley and Los Angeles, California

University of California Press, Ltd.
London, England

© 2010 by Terry Theise

Library of Congress Cataloging-in-Publication Data
Theise, Terry.
 Reading between the wines / Terry Theise.
  p. cm.
 ISBN 978-0-520-26533-2 (cloth : alk. paper)
 1. Wine and wine making—Miscellanea. I. Title.
 TP548.T48 2010
 641.2'2—dc22   2009050516

Manufactured in the United States of America

19 18 17 16 15 14 13 12 11 10
10 9 8 7 6 5 4 3

The paper used in this publication meets the minimum
requirements of ANSI/NISO Z39.48-1992 (R 1997)
(*Permanence of Paper*).

To Karen Odessa and Max

CONTENTS

INTRODUCTION

Some people will never learn anything, for this reason, because they understand everything too soon. —Alexander Pope.

I owe my life in wine to two people: Hugh Johnson and Rod Stewart.

Rod came first. It was a Faces concert at the late, lamented Fillmore East on Second Avenue in New York City. Somehow I'd scored a front-row seat. Faces concerts in those days were like big drunken ramshackle rehearsals, with lots of boozy bonhomie. Rod would swig from a bottle of Mateus Rosé, and on one occasion he passed it down to some twitching rocker in the front row, who took a greasy hit and passed it along. Then it got to me. First sip of wine. I *hated* it. Passed the bottle to the next guy. Finally the last hippie handed the bottle back to Rod, who pantomimed being seriously pissed off to find it empty.

Metamessage for me: wine is cool, rock stars drink it. I want to *be* a rock star. This was crucial information. I had to at least pretend to like wine.

Looking back all these years later, I see that this was the very moment wine, or the *idea* of wine, came to reside in my life. Not because I liked the stuff, but because I'd absorbed the idea that wine was crucial as a social-sexual marker.

As I grew older, I (and my girlfriend du jour) would often score a bottle of wine—most of which I hated—for a Saturday night. The first wine I ever drank and actually wanted to drink again was . . . (here go my credentials) *Blue Nun*. It was a novel feeling to enjoy drinking wine. It was a relief to drink something with low alcohol and fruitiness.

I'd lived in Munich, Germany, as a middle schooler; my father was head of the Voice of America's European division from 1965 through 1968. Those middle-school years are when you form your persona and self-image; the bands and clothes you like, what pack you prefer to run with (or which pack will have you). For me, this seminal time was forever connected to being in Germany, and I was eager to return someday. I took what purported to be a hiatus from college and went with my girlfriend to Europe, where we drove around in a severely beat-up old Opel we bought on the street.

After many months of wandering, we ended up back in Munich, since old family friends had told me the army usually had jobs available for civilian "components" of the Department of Defense, and of course we'd run out of money in a fraction of the time we'd imagined. This, improbably, is where Hugh Johnson comes in.

Our Saturday evening bottle soon morphed into our Friday *and* Saturday evening bottles, which in turn became Friday-Saturday-Sunday. We liked drinking wine more often—fledgling sybarites, you see. I shopped for wine each week, and all of it was supermarket plonk. Then three things happened.

I'd bought a random bottle we happened to like a whole lot, and when I went to buy more it was all gone, *ausverkauft*, never to return. The moral: when the wine's good, buy more fast. Thus was born a wine cellar, a terribly important way of describing our few dozen bottles on plastic store-bought racks. But any bunch of wine in excess of what you're drinking right now is a de facto cellar, and now I had one.

Second, I bought a bottle of something called "Riesling" for the first time. This was different! I had never tasted a wine with so *much* flavor that wasn't "fruity." It tasted like mineral water with wine instead of water. I needed to know what this odd new thing was.

One of our benefits was access to the army library, and one of the books in the army library was, yes, Hugh Johnson's *World Atlas of Wine and Spirits.* "The pictures are pretty, in case I can't deal with all these words," I reassured myself. But what words they were! Open to any page and there was something, an urbane turn of phrase, a stray bit of poetry, and, most striking to me, an unabashed emotionality. The Saar (which I could reach in a few hours' drive) "makes sweet wine you can never tire of: the balance and depth make you sniff and sip and sniff again . . . every mouthful a cause for rejoicing and wonder."

Rejoicing and wonder? All right, I can see rejoicing; I mean, after all, there's a moment of rejoicing in the first bite of a perfect cheeseburger if you're alert to it. But wonder? Was there more to this whole wine thing than I'd imagined? Was wine an object of beauty?

So I set about locating the wines Johnson wrote about, as best I could, and as best I could afford. I tried to taste them more attentively, to see whether they spoke to me. Sometimes they did, and sometimes I was groping. But the pictures in the book sure made wine country look pretty. Maybe it was time to see for myself.

And since we lived in Germany, and since these were the days before German wine became uncool, German wine country was the shortest distance from us. Armed and provisioned with maps and lists of recommended vineyards and producers, off we went. We parked at the edges of many wine villages, and went knocking on winegrowers' doors.

I don't suppose many of the growers we visited had ever been dropped in on by some hirsute freak with a list of geeky questions and a minuscule budget. But to my immoderate good fortune, then and many times since, I found German wine-growers to be *the* most generous and hospitable people I'd ever encountered. If you were interested and curious, there were few limits to the time they'd take or the samples they'd pour. If I asked about vineyards, they'd grab my arm and walk me up into the hills, explaining minutiae of geology and microclimate; if I asked about vintages, out came the bottles and the corkscrew. I protested lustily, but for naught. I said I needed to buy small amounts of a lot of *different* wines so that I could learn by survey-ing, to which they answered, Buy what you buy, it's no problem.

My entire world changed. It was May 1978, and I had found the thing I didn't know I was seeking. Or it had found me.

Wine, I discovered, could indeed be a thing of beauty. It could make you feel. It was endlessly changeable, and it played ever-wonderful variations on its themes; it wasn't just lovely, it was *interesting*. It was made in beautiful countryside, by sweet-natured people. And in many wines there were flavors I couldn't begin to account for. Music was similarly evanescent, but music's effects could usually be described; happy, sad, eerie, morose, pastoral, ecstatic, tender . . . but wine? What was going on here?

I lived five more years in Europe and visited most of its important wine regions, spent far too much money on wine and far too much time obsessing over it, not to mention boring the eyelashes off anyone around me if, God forbid, the subject of wine came up. We are all a little insane when we're infatuated. But my run of good luck continued; I experienced each new wine region by actually being there, absorbing its vistas, smells, horizons, whether the dogs were on leashes or roaming free, if it seemed welcoming (like Burgundy) or austere and taciturn (like Bordeaux), and I did this with Johnson's (and others') prose playing background music in my mind. There is no better way not merely to learn but also to *know* about wine. I belonged to no tasting groups, attended no wine classes. There was no Internet with its bulletin boards and exchanges of geekery. I did it alone and feverishly. My girlfriend became my first wife, Tina, and she was a very patient woman. Wine, for me, became something most vitally *intimate;* only later did it become something I connected to social life and conviviality.

I was driven to write about it long before I had anything of value to say. I liked to write; it seemed to complete my experiences, both of individual wines and of wine in the abstract. Somewhere in a dusty old shoebox is a primitive manuscript of a wine book I had no business producing. I could find it, but I doubt I could bear to read it. Yet even that early need to catalog information and describe experience was helpful, not least when

I cannibalized sections of the book into magazine pieces for an American journal called *Friends of Wine*. They paid me! Spent the first check on wine, of course; 1970 Montrose and Las Cases, as I recall. Finally opened the Montrose after staring at it nostalgically for twenty-six years.

In early 1983, when I returned to the United States after ten years in Germany, I wanted a job in the wine business. Suffice it to say I made my way. My progress was hardly picaresque; it was tedious. But it was progress. I put together a little portfolio of German wines from most of my old friends. Years later I helped introduce the splendid new wines of Austria to the States, and, undeterred by the indifference and derision that had become my daily lot, I assembled a slew of small Champagne growers to sell to the wary trade, effectively strapping a safe to my back to add to the grand piano already there as I pushed my rock up an endless hill. I seem to have had a fiendish gift for selecting uncool wine categories. For reasons still obscure, German wine was dead in the water in the mid-eighties. Nine years later, no one had heard of Austrian wine except that they put antifreeze in it some time ago. And *no one* believed they could sell "noname" Champagne.

It's not that I relished a challenge; I just wouldn't shrink from one. But I didn't go looking for weird or difficult wine categories, I just followed my odd little bliss. Years later, when interviewed for a magazine profile, I was asked, "So how does it feel to have perennially unpopular taste?"

"Just lucky, I guess," was my reply then, and it still would be today.

In June 2008 I received the James Beard Award for outstanding wine and spirits professional, our industry's equivalent to an Oscar. As I accepted the award I flashed back on those first formative years, overwhelmed with all I'd been given. This book will tell you how I got from those early quiet walks through remote, hilly vineyards to the longer-seeming walk onto the stage at Avery Fisher Hall after my name was called. It's time to give back. It's time to tell what wine can mean in a person's life.

But to do this I have to ask you to accept the ethereal as an ordinary and valid part of everyday experience—because the theme of this book is that wine can be a portal into the mystic. And we hate the very thought of the mystic, which seems so esoteric and inaccessible. But it isn't; it happens all the time.

A batter in a slump says (as one of my hometown Orioles did, just this morning), "It's like the ball is invisible." Another batter on a tear says, "I'm seein' the ball real good." Well, just what is happening here? It isn't mechanics; hitters and their coaches are seasoned professionals who know the basics. How does one describe these states of being in or out of "the zone"? I think we start by trying to describe what "the zone" itself is. And you can't do that without recourse to the mystic.

Musicians will sometimes reach zones of their own, often saying something like "I felt like a vessel through which the music was playing, as if I weren't generating it at all." And since that state exists but we don't know how to access it, what is its nature, and how do we find our ways to it?

My central argument is that wine can be a bringer of mystical experience—but not all wine. There are prerequisites, and I'll discuss them. In addition, there are collateral benefits to allowing oneself to be prepared for wine's mystical capacity. We also become sensitized to wine's *fun* capacity. But what is the process of cultivating this preparedness? That has been the subject of millions of words on Eastern thought, but when has it ever been applied to wine?

It begins with understanding what a "palate" actually is, and how to truly know one's own. It continues with cultivating a particular approach to wine, whereby one prefers the finer over the coarser virtues, the quiet over the noisy.

The ethereal can be forbidding when it isn't grounded in counterpoint to the ordinary. I wish this book to be ethereal, since it is defending the mystic, but I don't want it to be slack or nebulous. Neither do I want it to be too linear, though, because I don't hold that all experience is reducible to logic. I understand the difficulty of using language to describe evanescent or ineffable states. But instead of surrendering vaporously ("such things are beyond words . . ."), I'll confront the very limitations of language itself by asking what purpose it serves.

If you want to experience wine with your whole self—not only your mind and senses—the wine has to be authentic. And what confers authenticity is a rootedness in family, soil, and culture as well as the connections among them. These are aided by intimacy of scale. And they form the core of a value system by which *real* wine can be appreciated and understood.

Part of advancing this point of view is to identify what opposes it. It cannot suffice only to find the good and praise it, because the good is under ceaseless threat from the bogus and ostentatious. This tension forms the basis for a large quarrel between two sorts of wine drinkers, and they don't always play nice. I'll try to help us steer a decent person's way through.

I was fortunate to learn about wine in the best possible way, in the Old World among the vines and in the company of the families who grew them. One could call this a "classical" education, to learn the benchmarks of the subject firsthand, to place in the center what belonged in the center, and to appreciate the borders between the central and the peripheral.

In the end I'll share a few wine experiences with you, which will put these principles inside an actual life with wine.

If the text seems to meander or to sometimes repeat itself, I don't mind; in fact, I hope it does. It is less a strict cerebral argument and more a piece of a lifelong incantation. At times I might frustrate you by defining terms you already know, or failing to define terms you don't know. The actual you won't always be congruent with the many hypothetical yous I've had looking over my shoulder. I beg your pardon in advance.

Although this is not a wine primer, if I were an educator, the first thing I'd tell you is this: anyone learning about wines should begin in the Old World, where wine itself began. It's more grounded there. All things being equal, it is more artisanal, more intimately scaled, humbler, and less likely to be blown about by the ephemeral breezes of fashion. Its wines are made by vintners who descend from other vintners, often for a dozen or more generations. They are not parvenus, arrivistes, or refugees from careers in architecture, dermatology, software design, or municipal garbage disposal systems. They don't know about the wine "lifestyle," and if you tried to tell them, you'd likely draw a blank stare. You won't see a huge white stretch limo pulling out of their courtyards like the one I saw emerging ostentatiously from Opus One in the Napa Valley last year (I doubt it would *fit* in Ürzig or Séguret or Riquewihr or Vetroz). You'll never find *Bon Appétit* taking pictures in these growers' kitchens or at garden parties on the grounds.

Starting with Old World wines is also useful because they

don't do all the work for you. Non–wine people will wonder what I mean. Climate change notwithstanding, Old World wines (especially north of the Alps) have about them a certain reserve. They're not aloof, but neither are they extravagant, gregarious, life-of-the-party wines. They don't play at top volume, and they can seem inscrutable to people with short attention spans. They are, however, kinetic; they draw you in, they make you a participant in the dance. They *engage* you. They won't let you be passive, unless you choose to ignore them—in which case, why buy them? Yes, of course, I'm painting in broad strokes, but I won't clutter the prose with qualifiers; this is what I believe. Old World wines ask you to dance *with* them; New World wines push you prone onto a chair and give you a lap dance, no touching.

Other writers have clarified the disparate paradigms of Old and New World wines, and the rule of generalities applies; they are never more than generally true. Yet they exist for a reason. Notwithstanding the various honorable exceptions, New World wines are marked by a kind of effusiveness that turns the drinker from a participant into an onlooker. These big, emphatic wines put on quite a show: explosions and car chases in every glass. If you're new to wine, this can be reassuring. You get it. You needn't worry there are subtleties you don't grasp. But eventually such wines begin to pall.

Most New World wines cue off an Old World benchmark. The original is the great novel; the newbie is the made-for-TV movie based on the great novel. Not only is the complexity of the story squandered, but the entire experience of receiving it shrinks to a passive "entertainment" and obliterates the vital, breathing, imaginative life we bring to the act of reading.

Go on, call me opinionated! I accept it. But also call me a

man who stands for something. The alternative seems to be to stand for nothing, and that won't do.

I'm sitting at my dining room table with a glass of wine. On the walls around me are all the pieces of art I've collected. Laughably, these are mostly prints from calendars, but in my own defense they're Old World calendars with superior print quality! The scenes are all *peaceful;* they show cows, ponds, cows grazing near ponds, ponds reflecting the faces of cows, all these theta-wave-inducing scenes for which a city boy hungers. I have a stray thought: what will my son make of these? How will he remember them? Will they grow nostalgic for him; will he love them in retrospect? (I'm sure he finds them seriously boring right now.) My folks had a reproduction of a van Gogh that showed sailboats on a shoreline. It's probably famous. I saw it constantly when I was a kid. If I see it now, some kind of membrane grows permeable inside me. I don't even *like* the painting. But I'm plunged back into old, familiar waters. It's not associated with any discrete memory: I don't link it to my father burning the lamb chops or my mother cracking us all up. It is the sum of all the ethereal memory of being little, all the mystery of what I didn't know then and will never know, all the mystery of what becomes of the time, all the longing for what might have been said, said better, done better, how we might all have been better, starting with me. Sad, wondering, uneasy, oddly sweet.

Wine can talk to this thing in us. Some call it soul. Wine is not apart from this being within us. It doesn't have to be. It fits in tidily, and takes its place. All it needs is a soul of its own. It can't be manufactured; it can't have been formed by marketers seeking to identify its target audience. It needs to be connected to families who are connected to their land and to working their land and who are content to let the land speak in its own voice. Wines like this are valid because they don't insist you leave 90 percent of yourself at the rim of the glass. This trait stands apart from how good they are; that comes after. Plenty of wine can be contrived to bring you to a kind of peepshow of flavor, if that's your idea of a good time. *True* wine takes its legitimate place as part of your entire, true being. You are complete and human. You have not been reduced to a consumer unit whose behavior can be anticipated.

I didn't know any of this in 1978 when I started. No one explained it. I was shocked later on when I saw that wine could be otherwise, could merely entertain with its noise and phony seductiveness. Wine, it seemed, could be just another thing, *product*, disconnected from any reason a human being should care about it. My spirit felt starved when the caring wasn't there. I found the any-old-soil, technical nirvana New World ideal to be vacuous and lamentable. And yes—*of course*—there's no end of schlock from the Old World, but the Old World is hospitable to meaningful wine in a way the New World hasn't yet attained. A couple hundred years from now, it'll be a different story. Or so I hope.

In the pages to come I will challenge many common fallacies about wine, and I will show how wine can enrich your life by describing how it enriched mine. This isn't any sort of challenge to you, innocent reader. I've always cringed at the self-help "wisdom"-dispensing swamis for the rebuke underlying their message: *You live these pathetic, suffocating lives because you're not as smart as I am, but I'll consent to get you smart for $18.95 and a donation to my ashram in Boca Raton, Florida.* One of the great things about wine is that it will meet you wherever you manage to be.

I want to give you choices, and you can swallow what works for you and spit out the rest. I will make the case that wine belongs in a life of the soul, in an *erotic* life (in the Greek sense of *eros* as the force of life), but to encounter it there you have to be unsentimental and willing to demand authenticity from the wine and from yourself.

This doesn't guarantee exalted experience. It guarantees *real* experience. It guarantees that you won't have to curtail any aspect of your humanity to have a relationship with wine.

When my son was old enough to wonder what Daddy did, I had a hard time feeling satisfied with the answer that Daddy sold wine. I tried expanding it by explaining that Daddy sold wine he himself tasted and chose, but even then it seemed pretty mingy. Daddy sells stuff. Doesn't matter how adorable it is: Pop's a salesman.

How then does one define the larger questions? Is it even possible? It seems as if it must be, since I feel so stratified all the time. One layer is the garden-variety mercantile wine guy dealing with all the "issues" surrounding the zany categories with which I work. Everyone in the wine biz knows those issues: education, marketing, perseverance, dog-and-pony shows, "working the press." I try to be good at those things, or as good as my fallibilities allow. The other (perhaps deeper) layer is less concerned with the job and more concerned with the *work*. I have a voice in my head that always says, "Yes, *and?*" So if I ask myself what is the net effect of what I do, this voice propels me through ever more big-picture considerations.

I sell wine. *Yes, and?* I help ensure the prosperity of good artisanal winegrowers. *Yes, and?* I contribute to the continuing existence of cultures *containing* small artisanal winegrowers. *Yes, and?* To remain sustainable, I need to tell people why this is a good thing. *Yes, and?* In telling people why this is a good thing, I have to detail the reasons, which compels thoughts of soil, of family (the two are often combined into the word *terroir*), of a person's proper relationship with nature and to his human history. In short, I have to assert *values. Yes, and?* In delineating these values, I find I can't escape matters of soul. *Yes, and?* If soul enters the equation, you can't select what it inhabits, because soul inhabits either all of it or none of it. So what I finally end up doing is placing wine in the context of a life of the soul. *Yes, and?* So now I am defending and delineating the idea of living with conscience, gratitude, eros, humor, all the things soul imbues us with. And further, I'm placing wine squarely within this matrix and insisting that we don't have enough time to settle for less. *Yes, and?* And we seem to need certain things: to know where we are. To be connected to something outside ourselves. To be connected to something *inside* ourselves. And the only wines that actually speak to our whole lives are *authentic* wines, which are themselves both located and connected. Confected wines are not designed for human beings; they are designed for "consumers." Which do you want to be?

one

BEFRIENDING YOUR PALATE

First you master your instrument. Then you forget all that shit and just play.
—Charlie Parker, when asked how one becomes a great jazz musician

You're at home watching TV in the evening. Let's say you're watching a DVD of something you really like. Unless you have some monstrous home-theater system, you're looking at a relatively small screen across the room. You can't help but see all your stuff strewn about. Usually you have a light or two on. You hear ambient noises.

Now pretend you're at the movies. The lights go down, and you're sitting in a dark room with a bright screen encompassing your whole field of vision. Even with others around you, there is a strange, almost trance-like intimacy between these huge, bright images and your emotions. All great directors are acquainted with this spell; it's the essence of cinema. And it arouses a deep, almost precognitive attention from us.

We often think of palate as our physical taste receptor, the mouth itself, and, more saliently, the sense of smell. But a palate is more than what you taste; it is your *relationship with* what you taste. Palate isn't passive; it is kinetic.

Palate is really two things. First, it is the quality of attention you pay to the signals your taste receptors are sending. Second, it is memory, which arises from experience. A "good palate" is able to summon the cinema type of attention. An ordinary palate—more properly called an *indifferent* palate—is watching TV with the lights on.

Most of us are born with roughly the same discrete physical sensitivities to taste. (But there are said to be so-called super-tasters who may have a larger number of taste buds than the rest of us do, in which case, lucky them; they're getting bombarded with signals.) What varies is our sensitivity to this . . . sensitivity. It seems to be an irreducible aspect of temperament, how the gods arranged the goodies in the box called you.

I remember when I was a wine fledgling being complimented on my palate by people more experienced than I was. It wasn't as gratifying as it may seem. I had no idea what a good palate was supposed to entail. I guess it was good that I had one. Then what?

Later, when I taught wine classes for beginners, I did a little exercise at the beginning, putting four different brands of tortilla chips on numbered plates, and asking the eager wine students (who must have been wondering when their refund checks would be mailed) to taste all four and write down which one they liked best and why. A lively discussion never failed to ensue: "Number three has the deepest corn flavor" or "Number one wasn't salty enough" or "The taste of number four lasts the longest time." When it was all over I'd say, "Okay, guys, now you know everything you need in order to become good wine tasters." *Ah, excuse me?* But these students tasted variations on a narrow theme; they paid attention because they had to, and they put their impressions into words. They were *tasters*, and the medium didn't matter.

Yet the approach path to wine seems so fraught (compared to tortilla chips!); there are so damnably *many* of them, they change all the time, and just when you think you're getting a handle on the whole unruly mess you read about yet another obscure place entering the world wine market with labels that look like anagrams without enough vowels. It's dispiriting; I feel your pain. But you're completely wrong.

When I started my wine life I made the same mistake. I imagined some theoretical point of mastery that lay on the horizon, and I would reach it eventually if I just kept walking. But horizons are funny: they keep moving just as we do. The more urgently you walk, the more they recede. Bastards, mocking me like that; don't they know I'm *tryin'* here? Sure they know! They're just going to keep frustrating me until I finally get the message: enjoy the journey, and notice your surroundings.

But aside from this corner-store Zen wisdom, here's a practical suggestion: If the sheer cacophony of wine cows you, just ignore it. For at least three months—ideally even longer—choose two grape varieties, a white and a red, and drink *nothing but those*. Let's say you chose Sauvignon Blanc and Syrah. First you drink all the Sauv Blanc you can lay your hands on, California, New Zealand, Austria, all the various Loires, Alto Adige, and Friuli; you steep yourself in Sauvignon, seeing how the wines differ and what core qualities they all seem to have. Write each impression down. Do the same with Syrah: Australia, Rhône valley, Languedoc-Roussillon, California. When you start getting antsy for change, that's when you're ready for the next duo. You're getting bored with Sauvignon and Syrah because they aren't surprising you anymore. But boy, do you ever know them. You know them in your bones and dreams. Your very breath smells like old saddles and gooseberries.

Let's say you opt for Pinot Blanc and Cabernet Franc for your next duo. Right away you'll notice the newness of these wines, not only *that* they are different, but *how* they are different. You've immersed yourself in those first varieties, and every subsequent variety will automatically be contrasted with them. To know wine, learn its elements deeply and deliberately. Then your knowledge will be durable and your palate's vision will inexorably widen. Trying to skim over hundreds of different wines all at once will only make you cross-eyed.

This is hard for most of us because of all the many wines coming at us. Trust me, though: it's mostly static, and if you really want to learn you'd best find a system, or use mine. It builds your knowledge slowly, but what you build stays built.

The palate is an instrument played by the taster, and you're practicing and doing your exercises until you become facile. When that finally happens you think you've attained your goal, but you're still in a primitive zone of merely demonstrating the mastery you have obtained by practice and repetition. Eventually, if the gods consent, you stop worrying about *how* and start worrying about *what*. You forget about playing your horn (or your ax in my own mangy case) and just start to play the *music*.

You go to a party in a house you've never been to, and they have a really cool dog. You like dogs. But this particular dog is introverted or bashful, and the more you approach, the more he backs away. All you want to do is scritch him! But looks like it isn't happening, so you merge back into the throng and forget about Towser. Later you're sitting talking with some fetching young thing and suddenly you feel something cold and wet on the back of your hand. Well, look who's there: it's old Towser, sniffing you, checking you out. *Now* you can scritch his handsome head all you want. Scritch away—what a good boy! You go back to complaining to your friend about how no matter how much you study wine, it doesn't seem to get any easier. . . .

Wine is like a shy dog. Lunge for it and it backs away. Just sit still and it draws nearer. Wine is less about what you can grasp than about how you can *receive*. You grasp it more firmly if you grab it less tightly. It will resist you if you insist on subduing it. You can accumulate only so much knowledge in quantifiable bits, but you accumulate *understanding* if you learn to relax. Wine doesn't like being dominated. It prefers being loved and wondered about. It will do anything for you if you're curious and grateful.

I learned this the hard way, and so will you, if you don't already know it. I made quite an ass of myself strutting with my sexy-pants wine knowledge, and I wasted far too much time arguing with other wine geeks to prove my alpha cred. Learn from my sad past! The first hint I can offer is to try to distinguish between true complexity and mere complicatedness. The latter is usually frustrating, but the former is usually wonderful. You have to direct a beam of mind to pick a way through complicatedness. You set your jaw and grind your teeth until you've prevailed. You've nailed the flavors, quantified and named every nuance, and decided precisely how much you liked the wine on whatever scale they told you to use. But complexity asks the opposite. It is an immediate sense of something you *can't know*, something you won't be able to isolate or explain. Complexity is quiet; complicatedness is noisy. With complexity you have to relax your mind and see what happens. I can't promise this mental state is available to most of us, unless you are the Dalai Lama, until you reach a certain . . . ahem . . . age. It has been years since I worked *at* wine. I work *with* it, of course, and it's fun work, but I'm sure that after a certain point, the more we work at our pleasures (we say we "pursue" our pleasures, tellingly), the more they'll back away from us. Show me someone who "plays hard" and I'll show you someone who has forgotten how to play at all.

Of course, it *is* play, for many of us, to deconstruct and describe all of a wine's elements. But to the extent that they can be detected, what we're describing is intricacy, not (necessarily) complexity. A wine is complex when it suggests something that can't be seen or even known, but it is definitely, and hauntingly, there. A complex wine seems to channel the very complexity of living. A complicated wine is just a mosaic we piece together with our senses.

Here's what I think you're after: a point of utter receptivity in which you're seeing only the wine instead of seeing *yourself* seeing the wine. Oh, it does sound very Zen. But I'm persuaded it's the way to pleasure and sanity. If you don't see past your own discrete palate, you can't get past *What am I getting from the wine?* It starts and stops with "I." What am *I* getting, what do *I* think, how many points will *I* give it—all I can say is, if you drink wine this way, I sure hope you don't make love this way, because your partner's bored.

I know how it is; you're trying to get a handle on wine, and so you grasp for a handhold. If you're drinking a wine you like and someone tells you it was fermented with cultured yeast, the lightbulb goes on over your head: *Aha!* Cultured yeast = wine I like, thus I must posit the theorem that better wines are made from cultured yeast. Innocent enough. The problem arises when you cling to your belief despite any new evidence. It's tempting to add knowledge nuggets to your basket, and discouraging to chuck them away. But you have to; wine will force you to. It will lie in wait the minute you get certain about something, and trip you up in front of your friends, your sommelier, and the date you hoped to score with. Not that this has ever happened to me personally. . . .

It's actually best when you make a mistake. And the easiest mistake is thinking you've got it aced, because now you're not asking questions anymore, you're waiting for each wine to confirm your conclusions. Yet wine will contrive to confuse your assumptions in order to force you to still your ego and listen. If you hold wine too tightly, it can't dance with you. Hold it just right and it will glide over the floor with you as if you were a single body.

Remember, your palate isn't a thing you possess; it is part of you. You don't taste with this thing; you taste with your whole self. Some years ago there was a story about a so-called Robotongue the Japanese had developed, a machine that could be programmed to identify wines based on predictable markers (acidity, sweetness, and tannin, among others) and that was able to "perform" with uncanny accuracy. So the actual physiochemical reception of flavor can be bettered by a machine, which can register and catalog what it "tastes." But does it actually *taste?* We are entire human beings tasting wine; we bring our memories and longings and anticipations to every glass.

Each of us relates to our palates based on our temperament: a geek will have a geeky relationship with his palate, a right-brainer will have an elliptical and inferential relationship with his palate, and a linear, cataloguing person will organize his palate like a well-oiled machine. No single system is "best"; it's important to have the relationship that comes naturally. If you try to force it, you'll be doomed to frustration.

These relationships change over time. In a wine lover's early days, he's usually (and usefully) an obsessive note-taker. Notes help hone his powers of concentration and help him remember what he has tasted. My closets are laden with dusty old notebooks so full of entirely tedious tasting notes that my wife's running out of space for her shoes. She's right, I probably ought to chuck 'em. I hardly write notes anymore unless the wine is seriously moving. And I'm confident I can deconstruct a wine's flavor if I have to. In the early days I wasn't, none of us is, but like every muscle, this one got stronger the more I used it.

The greatest wines are the ones you can't write notes about because you're weeping, overcome with their loveliness. This happened to me in a restaurant in Paris one evening; the waiter must have thought my wife had just told me she didn't love me anymore and was absconding with the plumber. Nah, it was just the damned Jurançon. This, like all wine experiences, will jump out of the darkness at you, but it's okay, it's part of the spell. Don't fear the weeper.

There's no need to posture with your palate. Unless you publish tasting notes for a living, no one knows what you think or feel about the wines you drink except you. So don't play games. Don't grope for extravagant language, don't confuse what you admire or find interesting with what you spontaneously *like*, and please, if the wine smells like roses, it doesn't make you a better taster if you find some esoteric flower like buddleia to compare it to. Trust any impulse that emerges spontaneously, as these are most authentically *you*. Some wines intrigue with their mosaiclike arrangement of nuances, and it's fun to root around and glean the intricacy of the design. Other wines seem to be pure image. If you're at all in the synesthesia continuum you'll find color images come to you immediately. I definitely receive some wines as "green" or "orange" or "purple," and while some of this is reassuringly literal—purple as aromas of irises, wisteria, lavender, violets, for example—other times I have no idea why a wine seems "silvery" or why it might play in a "major" key. I just know the image makes sense even if I can't make sense of it. Your notes should help you remember not only how the wine tasted, but what it was like to drink it.

And what of the notorious practice of blind tasting? What, indeed.

For some people it is the sine qua non of wine knowledge. Many of the exams for various wine titles (Master of Wine, famously) require proficiency at blind tasting. Why, I don't know. Once a guy can bench-press three hundred pounds, he needs a way to employ that strength; otherwise, he can show off his irrelevant prowess only on the bench. Blind tasting as such is hardly a skill that will be put to use in a wine career, unless you plan to make a living playing parlor games with wine. Importer and author Kermit Lynch said it best: "Blind tastings are to wine what strip poker is to love."

Let's come back to the musical instrument metaphor. The palate is an instrument played by the taster. As you learn your instrument, you practice exercises and repetitions until you are skilled. Then it comes naturally. You don't get on a stage and play your exercises in front of an audience, and blind tasting is the equivalent of playing scales: valuable, necessary, but not to be confused with playing *music* or tasting wine.

When Keith Jarrett recorded *The Melody at Night, with You*, he was recovering from chronic fatigue syndrome. He couldn't play concerts; sometimes he could barely even sit at the piano for more than a few minutes. The CD is a recital of standards and folk melodies, played very straight, with little embellishment or technical bravura. The result is nearly sublime, tender, deliberate, caressing, essential, and pure. One time I answered the phone while the disc was playing, and as I walked back into the room I realized that if I'd been listening casually, I might have thought it was merely cocktail-lounge piano. Knowing the artist, his history, and the conditions under which the recording had been made gave it resonance and meaning.

What, then, is the value of reducing wine to a thing without context? What game is this we're insisting wine play along with? What's the *good* of tasting blind? Where's the silver lining of experiencing wine in a vacuum? Yes, it can train us to focus our palates and hone our powers of concentration. Then we can discard it! It has served its purpose. If we persist in tasting blind we run a grave risk—because it is homicidal to a wine's *context*, and wine without context is bereft of meaning, and the experience of meaning is too rare to be squandered.

But, you protest, blind tasting makes you objective! Oh, nonsense. Can anyone who has ever tasted blind really assert any pure motivation toward truth and objectivity, or does that person simply need to win the game by making the right guess? Besides, blind tasting will guarantee your "objectivity" only if this objectivity is so fragile it needs such a primitive crutch. If you're too immature (or inexperienced) to be objective when you have to be, blind tasting won't help you. It will, however, confuse you as to the purpose of drinking wine. And I'm not talking about only recreational drinking (remember *fun?*); the only genuinely professional approach to wine is to know as much about it as possible. Who made it, under what conditions, what are the track records of the site and the vintner—then and only then can a genuinely thoughtful evaluation of a wine take place in the fullness of its being.

I wish I could tell you how to hasten the process of relaxing into wine. But it takes the time it takes. It can't be forced. Here's how it was for me.

One morning I woke up thinking about a high school teacher I hadn't remembered in years. Jane Stepanski taught honors English, which I took as a junior. I had no great love of reading, but I had all the love I could stand for Mrs. Stepanski. Looking back on it now, we were an awfully fatuous bunch, and it's touching how she forgave us.

I needed the pack. I wasn't a nerd; I was what used to be called a "freak" exactly two years early. So I needed shelter, and honors English provided it, 'cause all the misfits were there. Oh, I read a little, but mostly I was earnest and clueless. I recall when my classmates were especially derisive of what they called truth-and-beauty poems. I went along with the prevailing contempt: truth-and-beauty poems—*ptui!* Only ignorant clods liked those. What kinds of poems did I like? Um, er, ah . . . well—*ahem*—um, y'know, all *kinds* of poems as long as they were *not* truth-and-beauty poems.

Looking back, what can you do but laugh? I don't disdain how we were, how I was. I was pitiable, I was so needy, we all were; we hungered for any scrap of certainty, any solid bit of floor to stand on, and so we struck our attitudes and Jane somehow didn't spit at us. She let us be, and was respectful, and steered us gently away from our silliness.

When I first got into wine in my mid-twenties, I was like every fledgling wine geek. It consumed my every hour, and sadly, it also consumed anyone in my proximity for a couple years. But I was greedy for knowledge, or rather for *information*, and I did what every young person does: I sought to subdue the subject by acquiring mastery over it. Ignorance was frustrating and uncertainty was actively painful.

Wine was behaving like the mechanical rabbit that keeps the greyhounds running the track. No matter how much knowledge I hoarded, the ultimate target remained the same distance away. The "truth" of wine, it seemed, was a sliding floor . . . and even then you had to gain access to the room. It frustrated my craving for certainty, for command and mastery. And for a time I was angry at wine.

Now I think it was wine that was angry at me. But as patiently as my old honors English teacher, wine set about teaching me what it really wanted me to know.

First I needed to accept that in wine, uncertainty was an immutable fact of life. "The farther one travels, the less one knows." There was no sense struggling against it; all that did was retard my progress toward contentment. But it is a human desire to ask why, to seek to *know*. Would wine always frustrate that desire as a condition of our relationship?

Far from it. But I was asking the wrong *why*. I clamored to understand "Why can't I know everything about wine?" But I needed to ask why I *couldn't*, why none of us ever can. Wine's essential uncertainty existed ineluctably, it seemed, and the most productive questions finally became clear: *What purpose does this uncertainty serve? What does it want of me?*

The first answer was quite clear: there wouldn't be one. There would, however, be an endless stream of ever more compelling questions. I often think you know you've asked the right question when the answer is an even deeper question. The "answer" is the end of the line. For me, answers were actually frustrating because they quashed the curiosity on which I'd learned to feed. It seemed, after all, to be questioning and wondering that kept my *élan vital* humming.

The less I insisted on subduing wine, the more of a friend it wanted to be. It let me understand that it was more responsive to love than to "knowledge." It showed me which came first, that knowledge derived from love and not from will. Wine is an introvert who likes his private life, I learned, and so I no longer had to seduce away its secrets with my desire to penetrate. The very uncertainty kept it interesting, and wine grew to be very fine company. These days I'm inclined to guess that wine's uncertainty wants to remind us always to be curious and alert to the world, grateful that things are so fascinating. And to be thankful for the hunger. Because the hunger is *life*. Accepting the irreducible mystery of wine has enabled me to immerse myself more deeply than I ever could when I sought to tame it.

Immersion is the key. I am immersed in the world, the world is immersed in me. There are filaments and connections, always buzzing and always alive. The world is not a commodity designed for my use; its cells are my cells, its secrets are my secrets. And every once in a while, usually when I least expect it, wine draws its mouth to my ear and says things to me. *Time is not what you think. A universe can live inside a speck of flavor. There are doors everywhere to millions of interlocking worlds. Beauty is always closer than it seems. Passion is all around us always. The brightest secrets play on the darkest threads. When you peer though the doorway, all you see is desire.*

You hear these words and maybe it all sounds like gibberish, a stream of sound that doesn't amount to anything and only confuses things more. But if you've ever held a restive infant, there's a little trick you can do. Babies like to be whispered to; it fascinates them. They get a wondering, faraway look on their little faces, as if angels have entered the room. And so I don't need to explicate what wine may be saying to me. It is enough that it speaks at all, enough that it leaves me aware of meanings even if these don't fall neatly into a schema; enough how sweet it feels, the warm breath of beauty and secrets, so soft and so close to my ear.

two

WHAT MATTERS
(AND WHAT DOESN'T)
IN WINE

H ave you ever tried to field the question, What kind of wine
do you like? Hard to answer, isn't it? At least it's hard to
answer briefly, because often the kind of wines you like need a
lot of words to describe them. I recently answered, "I like moderate wine," and I knew what I meant by it, though I'm sure my
questioner found me a tough interview.

Part of the business of deepening both your palate and your
acquaintance with your palate is to pay heed to what it responds
to. Eventually you organize that information as patterns mani-
fest themselves. These patterns are almost never random. They
tell you not only what you like and dislike, but also what you
believe in, what you cherish, and what you disdain.

I want to suggest a kind of charter of values by which we
enjoy wine, understand it, appreciate it, and place it in a matrix
of principle and judgment. I'm hardly qualified to do this for
"humanity," but I need to do it for myself, to locate where I am
at this point in my wine-drinking life. Test these ideas against
your own experience. Use what works, discard what doesn't,

create your own charter; in short, think about wine as something *ineluctably attached to your life*, not merely a diversion or entertainment.

Let's begin with how wines actually taste. It's the only reason to drink the stuff. It only *seems* imperative to our lives, but we can live without it. When we begin we drink wine because its taste is pleasurable, and indeed it remains so; it is only later (if at all) that we begin to realize we've formed a set of principles by which we've organized our wine experiences and learned to appreciate the many *forms* of pleasure.

Consider the following an attempt to codify a set of First Principles of Wine, starting with the way it tastes.

Aspects of Flavor: The Ones That Matter Most

Clarity
Distinctiveness
Grace
Balance
Deliciousness
Complexity
Modesty
Persistence
Paradox

These aren't the only aspects of flavor that matter, but when I delineate the relative importance of the things that make up Flavor, these matter most.

Clarity: Without clear flavors, none of wine's other aspects can be easily discerned. Clarity can connote brilliance, but it doesn't always; I think of the soft-lighted gleam of a Loire Chenin or dry Furmint, or the smoky evening-light depths of Barolo. But we should be able to see into a wine's flavor, even when it shows that which we *cannot* see. Clarity also suggests the work of an attentive vintner with a desire for candor and nothing to hide. For me it is the first of first principles. Flavor should be clear. The question of what the flavor is comes after. This is so obvious that no one considers it, but it is not self-evident. There are, distressingly, loads of blurry, fuzzy wines. I'm driven half-crazy if I'm riding in someone's car and he hasn't cleaned his windshield. Clarity!

Distinctiveness: Call it what you will—taste-of-place, terroir, "somewhereness" (author Matt Kramer's telling word)—but whatever you call it, it's the thing that says your glass contains *this* wine and no other, from *this* place and no other. Distinctiveness can include idiosyncrasies and quirks as long as they are spontaneous and not mere affectations. But it needn't imply quirkiness if it is a wine's innate nature to be classical and symmetrical. Some individuals are angular and others are rounded; what's crucial is that the *particular* is what shows. Distinctiveness makes a wine valid. The *Wine Advocate*'s David Schildknecht wrote, "Wines of distinction are wines of distinctiveness." The reason some of us are cool toward the "international consultant" school of winemaking—expert enologists-for-hire who fly around the world working their magic (and their formulas)—is that we feel these wines, no matter where they're grown, are stamped with a certain recipe, irrespective of what's at the market or in the pantry, so that we encounter big oak-aged ripe-fruited wine from this grape here and that place there, all melding into a big, bland glom. It's often an attractive glom, but how important is attractiveness, really? Should we pursue it at all cost? I don't believe we can even consider the question of "greatness" in wine until its uniqueness is established. I'll examine this question in more detail in a later chapter about globalization in winemaking. But suffice it to say, it's not enough for wine to have a passport; it needs a birth certificate. I'd rather drink something that tastes like *something* and not like everything. Anything can taste like everything, and too often does, and bores the crap out of me.

It's only a small digression to wonder at the whole international wine personage phenomenon, as it seems inimical to the rootedness that is inherent in authentic wines. I'm not sure why it's chic for someone to fly thousands of miles to make wine. I appreciate wanderlust, but I'm happier when people choose a place and make wine there, ideally the place they were born and raised. They then become linked to that place, and their wine expresses the connection. Otherwise wine becomes little more than a plaything. Don't misconstrue me; there's nothing morally wrong with making wine anywhere you please. I just don't think it's inherently fascinating or desirable. It rather adds to the incoherence of the world. And whatever it is, it ain't glamorous.

Grace: This quality can apply to wines of various degrees of strength, body, or ripeness, and it can be found in both polished and "rustic" wines. It allies to modesty, but not every modest wine is graceful. Grace is rather a form of tact, a kindness; it rejects coarseness and is even more dismissive of power merely for its own sake.

Balance (and its siblings, Harmony and Proportion): Balance is not to be confused with symmetry, as there are asymmetrical yet balanced wines. Balance is simply the palpable sense that no single component appears garish or inappropriate. It is a quality of flavor that draws you away from the parts and toward the whole. It is a chord of flavor in which no single note is out of tune. If you hear any one of its component notes, it's probably for the wrong reason.

In a balanced wine the flavors seem preordained to exist in precisely that configuration. You sit by the stream. The water is clean and cold. The mountain peaks are clear. There are no beer cans or cigarette butts in sight. You've been hiking for a few hours and you feel loose and warm and hungry. You unpack your lunch and take the first bite, and then you see your sweetheart coming up the path, smiling. The air is soft and cool under a gentle sun. Things are absolutely good. Happens, what, once in a lifetime? In a balanced wine it happens with every sip.

Deliciousness: It is strange to have to mention this, but deliciousness is hardly ever spoken of or written about. A wine can meet every other criterion for success and yet not *taste good*. Then what? Do we outgrow appreciating deliciousness? Do we cultivate more auspicious tastes? Well, poo on us. Deliciousness ignites something in us that delights at the scent of pleasure. Is it wise to quash this thing? What else dies with it?

Complexity (and its siblings, Ambiguity and Evanescence): There is *explicit* complexity, wherein each component of a wine can be discerned and we are delighted by how many there are and how they interact. There is also *implicit* complexity, in which we sense there is *something* present but oblique to our view. Finally, in the few best wines there is a haunting sense of *something being shown to us* that has nothing to do with discrete "flavor." This is the noblest of wine's attributes, but the hardest to contrive by design. It seems to be a by-product of certain vintners' philosophies and practices, but neither formula nor recipe exists; this aspect is found when it is found, often unexpectedly. Some wines are complex in themselves, and it stops there. Other wines seem to embody *life's* complexity, and this is when we see the view from the sky.

Modesty: This denotes a wine that seeks to be a companion to your food, your state of mind, or the social occasion, as opposed to a wine that needs to dominate your entire field of attention. Some wines deserve your entire field of attention, but they don't need to shout for it. Modest wines are endangered in these times, when power is overvalued. Just because your text is written in boldface doesn't mean you have anything to say. Modest wines are tasty, tactful, and confident, and they don't show off.

Persistence (and its siblings, Depth and Intensity): This attribute properly comes *after* the ones cited above, since a persistent unpleasant wine is no one's idea of fun. A good wine is elevated by persistence, a bad wine diminished. Nor does persistence have to do with volume; the best wines are the ones that *whisper* persistently. We misunderstand the idea of intensity because we conflate it with volume. Bellowing flavor isn't intense; it's adolescent and irritating. Intensity arises not from a will to express, but from the thing that is being expressed.

Paradox: I can scarcely recall a great wine that didn't in some sense amaze me, that didn't make my palate feel as if it were whipsawed between things that hardly ever travel together. My shorthand term for that experience is *paradox;* again, this component is in the hands of the angels and doesn't appear susceptible to human contrivance, but when it is found it conveys a lovely sense of wonder: How can these things coexist in a single wine? And not only coexist, but spur each other on; power *with* grace, depth *with* brilliance. . . .

Aspects of Flavor: The Ones That Matter Least

Power

Sweetness

Ripeness

Concentration

It's not that these aspects don't matter at all, but too many think they matter too much. They appear near the bottom of my scale of values, but they do appear.

Power: Power matters only when you're planning a menu and selecting the wines. You want to align the power of the dish with that of the wine, so one doesn't subdue the other. But power inherently is a quality neither desirable nor undesirable; it needs to justify its existence by combining with grace, distinctiveness, and deliciousness. Too often it stops at mere incoherent assertiveness: I'm putting my fist through this wall *because I can!*

Sweetness: In the wine world there's no single component of flavor subjected to more obsessive dogma and doctrine. The prevailing (and I'd say *pathological*) aversion to sweetness has diminished many wines. Sweetness figures in menu planning and in forecasting the way a wine might age. It is sometimes helpful. Like acidity, tannin, or any other single facet of flavor, sweetness matters only when there is too much or too little of it. Yet we focus on it in isolation, insisting that it be reduced or removed at all cost, unaware that we are misguided and have taken balance, length, and charm away from our wines. Sweetness should be present when it is called for and absent when it is not, as determined by the flavors of individual wines and not by any theory we have promulgated a priori.

And a lot of us are confused about sweetness. I'm here to help. There's the sweetness of an apple, and there's the sweetness of a Twinkie. They're not the same!

Ripeness: I refer especially to *physiological* ripeness, sometimes called phenolic ripeness, which is seen when a grape's skins and seeds are ripe. It would seem to be desirable, but the singular pursuit of physiological ripeness as an absolute has wrecked many wines by condemning them to a power they can't support, and it has removed the nuance possible when wines are made from grapes of different degrees of ripeness. When ripeness is sufficient, how do we assume overripeness will be preferable? It only brings more alcohol and an infantile swaddle of fruit.

Concentration: Concentration matters only after this question is answered: What are we concentrating? Tannin, viscosity, alcohol? Are these things we want even more of? In itself, concentration is merely an adjective, not a virtue.

Taking a Stand: What Is Not Important

Why begin by discussing the unimportant? you might ask. Because these ephemera take up far too much of wine discourse, deflecting us from more important matters. I remember Gore Vidal's famous answer to the question of why academic quarrels were so fierce: because the stakes were so low.

You might expect the wine world to be a gentle and civilized place, but you'd be wrong. You'd think habitual wine drinkers would be less querulous than other folks. Wrong again. Then you'd get tired of always being wrong, and realize that wine can be a lightning rod for many other debates—or arguments—that are conducted with humanity's usual standards of skill, intellect, civility, and tolerance. In other words, it's Mailer versus Vidal, minus the erudition.

Important matters become obscured by opinionated posturing from people who've succumbed to the modern inability to distinguish conviction from pugnacity—not to mention the temptation to make simplistic intellectual fast food out of complex issues. I call them "thought Twinkies"; they masquerade as substance while offering only spuriously seductive assertion. I expect such things from beginners intimidated by the intricacies of wine, but some of the worst offenders are some very powerful elders of the wine world, who ought to know better, or *be* better.

Wine people get combative when they fear a threat to the existence of the kinds of wines they like. But combativeness becomes a habit, a default position for people unwilling to make the effort entailed by reasonableness. And suddenly every little nonissue is absurdly exacerbated by people staking claims on categorical positions. If we don't, we look, what—weak? We are often wrong, but never uncertain!

Don't mistake my meaning; there are many places where values belong, and when you're in such a place you're a coward if you don't assert yours. But when you're asserting value judgments over work you yourself don't actually *do*, you risk sounding fatuous. And the need to see wine merely as a warren of opportunities to decide rights and wrongs is a blind alley, and it hinders both knowledge and appreciation. I thus assert the value of knowing when asserting values is called for.

Here are a few of the prominent issues around which opinions orbit, beginning with the silly ones.

Yields: This issue is rife with truisms. The prevailing assumption is that you must have low yields in order to have any claim to quality. Ostensibly, it makes sense; the less fruit per acre, the more flavor in each bunch of grapes. But more flavor doesn't always equal *better* flavor. Our obtuse insistence that low yields will always give better wines has given rise to a community of clumsy, opaque, and joyless wines, overconcentrated, overendowed, just plain *overdone*. The simplistic equation—low yields = superior wine—is true only if *concentration* is the sole criterion of quality. But any good restaurant line cook knows how to reduce a sauce to just the right point, and he also knows what happens when you go too far. You get an opaque substance that's like a black hole from which no flavor can emerge. The entire matter of yields needs to be seen as a mosaic winemakers evaluate according to the kind of wine they wish to make. Sadly, when you dare to suggest this you'll get mocked by the lovers of forceful wine, as if their own bellicosity were validated by the wines they prefer.

They will accuse you of mounting an elegant rationalization for thin, anemic wines. And sometimes they are right. Other times they can seem obtuse to the value of transparency. Certain kinds of wine aren't meant to be "intense" and musclebound. Nor does each wine drinker enjoy the same things in wine. Some people like to be overwhelmed. I like my whelm the way it is. I don't like Hummer wines.

And when we earnestly measure yields in terms of hectoliters per hectare (or tons per acre), we're laughed at by most serious vintners, who know how those numbers can be fungible and manipulated. You can say you made your wine from fifty hectos per hectare, but maybe you actually grew seventy-five and sold off the excess twenty-five. Maybe your yields were low because your husbandry was lousy. Maybe your vineyard was sick with rots and mildews and when you finished picking out the healthy fruit your "yield" looked tiny. Yield per vine and vines per hectare get us closer to the truth. Seeing the question as an interface of economic sustainability for a vintner along with an appropriate—an *appropriate*—degree of concentration in his wines is more flexible and realistic. For proof that "high" yields can give lovely wines, consider the entire Mosel valley! Its yields seem high on paper, but the wines have the concentration they need, and no more. In fact, the entire region is in retreat from the era of ever-lower yields, as they learned they had too much overripe fruit, which led to shortages of the scintillating light Rieslings for which the Mosel is beloved.

Yeasts: I've witnessed fairly new wine lovers eager to make value judgments on this subject. They don't see the vintner snickering behind their backs. Mind you, the question of what yeast a grower uses to ferment his juice is interesting and worth discussing, but it is almost never decisive. Even so, it is perhaps a useful illustration of wine people's need to take categorical positions. Wine gets uncomfortably near to theology at such times, and it seems a pity to reduce this sensuous, civilizing being to a mere object over whose nonsalient details we squabble desperately. Still, in the context of a list of tangential matters that wine folk spend far too much time obsessing over, the last thing I need to do is indulge in obsessive detail to prove my point that detail isn't warranted! Still, maybe a little footnote-type diversion might prevent opacity. In that spirit, and do skip ahead the moment your eyes start glazing over . . . I present the Apostasy of the Yeasts!

Vintners have two options for fermenting their grape juice. Either they let nature do it for them—spontaneous or "ambient" yeast fermentation—or they inoculate their juice with cultured yeast. Within the latter choice lies a range of options. All yeasts form flavor, but some are more aggressive than others, and a case can be made that the most aggressive ones cross the line into confecting flavor not inherent in the grape itself. That is as far as I will go in suggesting a value judgment, and I'm not entirely sure of even this much.

Growers who use cultured yeasts usually do so in order to have a predictable fermentation, especially if their cellars are naturally cold and they want their wines to be dry. In some instances growers desire a very cold fermentation because they like the aromas that naturally result. Some tasters dislike those very aromas, which can recall pear drop or banana, but that is solely a question of taste.

The range of possible yeasts is greater than one might suppose. There are mass-produced industrial yeasts, and there are specific yeasts for certain grape varieties and also for highly concentrated dessert-wine musts. I know of several instances in which growers had cultures made from their own wild vineyard yeasts, and one of these growers went further and had variety-specific ones made, that is to say, a special yeast cultured from a vineyard in which only a particular variety was planted. And even among the commercial cultured yeasts are types that purport to be entirely neutral.

But there's a lot we don't know about the process, including what yeast actually starts a fermentation, because even if you inoculate, can you ever be certain it was *that* and not an ambient yeast that got the party started? It sounds laudable to culture one's own vineyard yeasts, but it has yet to be proved that it's anything more than a seductive romance to assume yeasts are a crucial, inherent aspect of terroir.

Assuming a grower has a conscience, he'll choose cultured yeast to create a certain texture and transparency in his wine and to avoid bacteriological or sulfide problems that would require technological interventions to solve. He chooses what seems to him a benign fermentation method up front so as to avoid a more serious agitation of the wine later. I know a great many growers whose methods are as rigorous as the most devout wine purist could require, yet they ferment with cultured yeasts.

What of the ones who go wild, as it were? In some cases it is part of an overall hands-off approach, which one can certainly appreciate as long as the wine tastes good. But in some cases it's an affectation; it gives growers a fashionable thing to say while at the same time they may be doing all kinds of things we might find unsavory. But let's posit a wild-yeast-fermented wine as part of a general tolerance of "naturalness" (if you approve), "funkiness" (if you disapprove), or "animalness" (if you approve of funkiness!). If you are an experienced taster, and I emphasize *experienced*, you might sense that the wine is unpolished, undeodorized, hewn a little more toward "country" rather than "city." Maybe you prefer the style. Fine! I like it, too. But I don't conflate it with All That Is Honest and Moral in viticulture. Surely we understand that persons of conscience do not make identical choices.

Each option for starting fermentation has advantages and disadvantages, and almost without exception none is "morally" preferable to another. I'm inclined to sympathize with growers who insist on letting their wine ferment spontaneously, but what am I to make of the many growers equally passionate about terroir who use cultured yeast? Are they disingenuous, misguided, ignorant, poseurs? Or am I just being a pill?

One grower told me, "There's entirely too much conversation about this really minor issue. I doubt if even experts could tell you which wine was fermented which way more than 5 percent of the time." And he's right. Yeast is almost never more than an *inflection*. But it has become a coat-hook upon which we hang all kinds of categorical value judgments. I suspect that ten years from now we'll look back and ask, "Why were they obsessing about yeasts in those days?"

Winemaking methods: Of course, these are significant in descriptive terms, but rarely in forming absolute judgments. Oxidative (vinification with oxygen encouraged) or reductive (vinification with oxygen discouraged); which is "better"? Steel or cask; which is "better"? Whole-cluster pressing or conventional crush-and-press; which is "better"? The answer—*always*—is *It depends*. The common risk we run is that we fall in love with an estate and learn how the vintner makes the wine, whereupon we conclude, *This must be the way to make great wine*. And we memorize the formula (if there is one) and think we've learned something. But I guarantee you that soon, very soon, you're going to fall in love with another wine estate that makes wine completely differently than the first one. Each vintner can defend his or her preferences with great conviction, yet the two methods are mutually exclusive. And you, poor you, are trying to suss out who's right. Sorry, but they're both right; it's you who's wrong. You don't have to choose! You just have to *pay attention*, consider, and understand what prods different vintners to make wines in different ways. It says something about them; what they like to drink, perhaps, or what they learned from their fathers. The value lies there, in human terms.

Taking a Stand: What Is Important

I'll outline my position here, and elaborate at length in subsequent chapters.

Artisanality: By this I mean a connection between the worker and the work made possible by intimacy of scale. I think this is a first principle, if only to establish a beachhead against the seductions of industrial, "product"-driven winemaking. This leads to . . .

Connections: Various connections are important: first, the connection of the vintner to his land (and the inseparable connection of flavor to that land); then the connection of the worker to the work; then the connection of the family to the culture of family estates; and finally, our own connection as drinkers to something we know is true, important, and worth defending and preserving. When we insist on these things as preconditions for attending to wine, we will know when they are absent, and the wine will lose its savor and its claim on our attention.

How the soil is treated: This one's a sticky wicket for people with an environmental conscience. How vineyards are treated is manifestly important. But it doesn't invariably follow that a continuum of "purity" exists upon which each vintner can be measured. And how could we presume to do the measuring? I take a dubious view of people who never had to support a family growing grapes and making wine preaching to those who do about living up to their precious purity standards. Between the total hack working with any and all chemicals at one extreme and the organic or biodynamic grower at the other, there lies a complex spectrum of values and possibilities. We need to attend as concerned and reasonable beings, but we do not need to assign points on some green-o-meter. What we should do is look and listen—to each grower's ambient conditions (dry versus humid, flat versus steep, among others) and to the values by which the grower works. Absolute judgments on our part are liable to be fatuous. We'll know a grower's conscience when we see it, and persons of conscience may make decisions different from those we *think* we'd make from our remove.

True flavor: This comes from the land, not from the cellar or from any of its bazillion possible treatments. Mosel grower Karl-Josef Loewen says, "In the modern world there are hitherto unimagined possibilities to form the tastes of wines. In my region there are people using *barriques*, using the most current techniques to concentrate natural musts, special cultured yeasts to form the characters of wine, and special enzymes to form bouquets. Is this the brave new wine world? I have a different philosophy." Bearing in mind that all viniculture is manipulation, it follows that we'd be better served attending to agitation, to anything that diminishes a wine's inherent vitality, and to any and all practices that add flavor not inherently there. Oak is the most blatant example, of course.

To the extent that a wine culture exists where it should and as it should, these things tend to apportion themselves properly. A simple example is Mosel Riesling: the vine clearly thrives in that land, the wines are holistically appropriate; a normal year, the grapes are *just* ripe enough while still laden with crisp, refreshing acidity. The wines convey an energy that corresponds to the effort needed to grow grapes on the killing-steep mountainsides.

If, in order to make potable wine, it must be subjected to manipulations bordering on (or becoming) falsification, then something is askew. Suppose I like golden retrievers, and say I live in a very hot climate, and say this breed of dog is extremely uncomfortable in very hot climates. Obviously I should get a different breed of dog. What I shouldn't do is to shave the poor bastard bald or give him some drugs to make his coat fall out. If you have to diddle your wine to remove the undesirable facets with which it was born (or that you brought about by insisting, among other things, on "physiological ripeness"), then you're not hearing what nature is saying: *You're growing the wrong grapes in the wrong place.* You're picking overripe grapes because you're scared they won't be "physiologically" ripe. Your wine has far too much potential alcohol, so you add water to the grape must. That takes color away, so you add it back with a compound called Mega Purple, an extract of grape skins. You also "adjust" alcohol by using spinning cones or reverse osmosis. For the drinker, to take a stand against such manipulated wines is to assert the value of the right thing grown where it belongs, and the distinctiveness and honesty of the results in the glass. Little enough to ask, it would seem; yet it is everything.

It's time to elaborate on one of this book's most crucial themes, which breaks down into three ideas: connectedness (the most important), attentions, and the thing to which the first two lead, artisanality.

Connectedness

I woke up this morning thinking about Germany's Mosel valley, and about a vintner family I know well, the Selbachs of Zeltingen. I first met them in 1985; it was Hans and his wife, Sigrid, in those days, with eldest son Johannes waiting in the wings. Hans died recently, and suddenly, and when I visit the Mosel each March to taste the new vintage, I pay a visit to his grave, which has a view of the silvery river and the village of Zeltingen, where he and Sigrid raised their family. Indeed, if the steep hill behind the St. Stephanus church weren't a cemetery, it would certainly be planted with vines, and Hans and his vines alike rest deep within the slate.

He died at home, surrounded by family. His body was carried through the house, through the bottle cellar (one of his sons told me, "Terry, it was as if you could see and hear the bottles stand and applaud Papa"), before it was placed at last in the ground, perhaps three hundred meters from the house. It is not only his spirit that lingers genially among his survivors; his body itself is near at hand.

My own father died abruptly. I was about to be a senior in high school. I came home one afternoon from my summer job and he was slumped over the kitchen table. He died six hours later in a hospital room while I waited at home with my small sister. He is buried in an enormous cemetery in Queens, New York; I doubt if I could even find the gravesite.

My story may not be typical, but neither is it all that unusual. We were suburban folk, and a certain existential disconnect was a defining parameter of our experience. Nor do I claim this is necessarily tragic. Disconnection has its silver linings if you're a lone wolf.

But when I contemplate the connectedness the Selbachs nurture and presume upon, it becomes clear that their wines are also connected, that *they* are a defining parameter in a complex of connections. This is as invisible and vital as oxygen to the Selbachs and people like them.

Johannes speaks nearly perfect English. In fact, he gets along in French and for all I know can mumble articulately in Chinese. What I didn't know, or had forgotten, is that along with his native German he also speaks *Platt*, or regional dialect. I heard him speak it when we visited another grower together. It was the Merkelbachs, two bachelor brothers now about seventy, who have barely ever left their village and who make a living from a scant five acres producing some thirty different casks of Riesling, each of which they bottle separately. As I heard Johannes lapse into dialect it struck me what a piece of social glue this was; it was Johannes's way of reassuring Rolf and Alfred, *We are brethren*, another marker of connection and identity. One might almost claim that Mosel Riesling is what it uniquely is because of the dialect *it* speaks.

I find I am *satisfied* in some essential way by connected wines. It doesn't even matter whether I like them. I happen never to have met a Priorat I enjoyed, but I respect Priorat for its authenticity—it is manifestly the wine of a place, speaking the dialect of the sere, barren terraces in northeastern Spain. I may not like it—I have issues with high-alcohol wines—but I'm glad it exists.

I can't summon up anything but weariness for the so-called "international" style of wine (ripe, "sweet" fruit, loads of toasty oak, a spurious seductiveness), since it's either connected to things I don't care about or connected to nothing at all. I've had more than enough disconnect in my life. Many of us have. When I consider a Mosel family like the Selbachs—like any of the people with whom I work—everything I see expresses an identity rooted in connection; they themselves, their wines. You could not disconnect these things even if you tried.

And it salves a kind of loneliness. Though it isn't my home, it is at least *a* home, and the people are particular people, and the wines are particular wines. I spend too much of my life driving among strip malls and their numbing detritus, and so when I descend the final hill over the Eifel and the village of Zeltingen comes into view, sitting peacefully along the Mosel, I have a momentary thrill of *arriving*. Here is *somewhere*. I see it, I know it, I will soon embrace people who embody it—and I also get to *taste* it.

I will not settle for less from any wine. Nor need you.

When I'm there I stay at home with the Selbachs, and since the family likes to eat and knows how to cook it is an ongoing challenge to maintain my trim, boyish profile. I need to tramp, ideally every day, and the surrounding vineyards are ideal for tramping, steep and beautiful. One morning I set off into the misty, moist freshness, with a high fog riding about five hundred feet above the valley. I stamped up to a trio of wild cherry trees blooming halfway up the Himmelreich vineyard. I pushed at top speed to get warm. Kept climbing. Got up into the woods too high for vines and listened to the birds fluting away, new birds with unfamiliar voices.

The Himmelreich hill leads back into a small combe that gives way to the next hill, corresponding to the Schlossberg vineyard, and this in turn leads southeast to the great Sonnenuhr. I was on a high path with the Mosel vertically beneath me through the vines, and only the woods above. Some workers were pruning and binding here and there, and it seemed lovely to be out on such a sweet, cool morning working with the vines in such pretty surroundings. I know very well it isn't always like this—these vineyards get hot in the summer, or grapes wouldn't ripen—but I seemed to have passed through a membrane, and everything was suddenly and clearly *divine*. The small teams of people working, the birds noisily peeping, the languorous Mosel below, the smells of slate and wet trees. These fugue states are so sudden; you just take a small step through what you thought was yourself, and you're in some silent, airy space that's strangely durable while you're there. I passed a group of workers replanting in the Sonnenuhr and bade them *Guten Morgen*, glowing and goofy with joy and certain we all were as giddy as I was.

But of course to them I was probably just another crazy tourist blown away by the view.

I turned to head back down and walked past Hans Selbach's grave, and I wanted to stop and talk to him, to tell him, *It's still like it always was, old friend; it's a beautiful foggy morning and the workers are working and the birds are birding and it's all as it should be, and you were right, it is divine and full of love and patience, this little bit of the world.* I got back late and my colleagues were waiting impatiently, but I didn't feel too bad; I'd burned a bunch of cals *and* had a mystical reverie—all before 10:00 A.M.

Visiting Hans isn't a duty; I need to do it. I love that he lies in the slate, the soil where his Riesling grew. I love that he views the village and the river. I love thinking of harvesttime, when the air will be full of the voices of the pickers and the thrum of the tractors, all nearby. Later the first snow will sift and settle over the graves where Hans and his neighbors lie in the slate above the river.

I think that we who love Mosel wine do so with a special tenderness. That is partly because of the wines' particular sparrowy charm, but if you have ever been there you find in these wines a taproot from which you can drink from your soul's purest waters. These wines do not merely hail from a culture; they're so deeply embedded in that culture you can't tell anymore where one ends and the other begins. The cohesion is both stirring and unnerving. Looking at the mourners at Hans Selbach's funeral, many of their faces could have been carved on Roman coins. They were the people of *this* place in the world. It's no accident that there are almost no international consultants, the "flying winemakers," from here. The Mosel gives its vintners all the stimulus they need.

Yet as much as I love this culture, I recognize its shadow side. It is not exclusively lyrical. If its air is rarefied, that's partly because it isn't always as fresh as it might be. There are all the petty jealousies and Hatfield-McCoy chicaneries that afflict small-village life around the world. But there is more.

I represent two Mosel producers who are neighbors on the same site; their parcels are contiguous. One producer hadn't quite finished picking grapes when his Polish harvest workers' work visas expired, meaning the crew had to return to Poland. No problem, said the neighbor; we'll pick for you. *We'll pick for you!* It really is another world. People may know one another for twenty years and still address each other as *Herr*-this and *Frau*-that. They have all the ratty bullshit that can possibly exist among people, but—"We'll pick for you."

Sigrid Selbach (Hans's widow and the matriarch of the family) told me a story once. "We picked our Eiswein last year on Christmas Day," she began. "The day before, when we saw it might be cold enough on Christmas morning, we hesitated to call and ask for help with the picking. But you know, we called twelve people, and they all agreed to help, and they were all *cheerful* to do it. We went out into the vineyard before dawn to check the temperature, then phoned them at 6:00 on Christmas morning, and they all came and all in a good mood. Afterward they gathered here at the house for soup and Christmas cookies. And when they left they were all singing out *Merry Christmas* as they went home to their families. Isn't that wonderful?"

I ask you! I too am amazed that people would cheerfully agree to get out of their warm beds before dawn on Christmas morning while their loved ones slept, to go out into the frigid vineyards and gather enough fruit for a few hundred bottles of wine that nobody makes any money on. This is more than mere neighborliness. It is simply assumed that certain traditions are ennobled by observing them with a hale kindness. When nature gives you a chance at an Eiswein, you *celebrate* the opportunity. Your grapes might have rotted or been eaten by wild boars. But this time the gods smiled.

Being a Mosel vintner signifies membership in a human culture much deeper than mere occupation. This is true of every vintner, whether his wines are great, good, or poor. This may seem abstruse to the "consumer," but there are many ways to consume and many things to *be* consumed in a glass of wine. You can see it merely as an object and assess it against its competitors using some arbitrary scale. Or you can drink something that tells you it was made by human beings who want to show you the beauty and meaning they have found in their lives. *You* decide.

A few years ago I saw a newspaper piece about a wine salesman who was realizing his "dream" by making wine—or "making wine"—in California. He owned no vines. The fruit he bought was crushed for him (they call it custom-crushing out there) by I don't remember whom. His winemaker was a hired gun out of U.C. Davis. All of this was unremarkable; it is the common and vapid story of much New World wine. Their first vintage was offered to the market for $125 per bottle (a small fortune in those days), and then I knew the world had gone mad.

Let's call such a wine Hubris Hill. The "producer" doesn't tend a vine or make the wine, doesn't even own a vine, but he's sure willing to claim your $125 because he knows how many suckers are born per minute, and how easily they'll pony up if the reviewers gush about the wine's *oodles of jammy hedonistic fruit erupting from the glass in subatomic orgasms of delirium: 95 points.*

This, we are led to believe, is wine. *Wine* (n)—anything anyone can contrive to make, detached from nature, detached from culture, connected to nothing but our infantile need to be entertained and our adolescent need to be fashionably correct, to be sold at the highest price that some desperate hipster can be horsewhipped into paying.

If this were the summit of wine's aspirations, I wouldn't shed a tear if it disappeared from the world. It feels as if we move through life in a fog sometimes. And when we alight on something real, someplace real, it's like putting on eyeglasses that suddenly show what's blemished and bogus around us. To me it is urgent that we recognize those things and avoid them. The bogus isn't good for us. It's like a sugar high that leaves us crashed and wretched later. We get confused, and lose our bearings.

But Mosel wine hails from someplace true in the world, and from the people connected to it and the culture they created, which honors the connection. Can we ever have too many reminders that such places persist? If you're sinking into ennui as yet another corporate type presses his marketing strategies on you, as yet another former dermatologist or veterinarian lords his milk-and-honey lifestyle over you and you wonder what any of it has to do with wine, with why you first fell in love with wine—I have places to show you. If you're weary of reading about grape-skin concentrates and oak chips and spinning cones and must concentrators and debt service and consultants who guarantee a certain critic's score—if you're weary of even thinking about scores—I have places to show you.

If you read a passage of poetry and feel that sudden silence as the world expands and deepens, and you hear yourself wonder, *I used to have this thing in my life; where did it go?* I have places to show you. They are what I wish to capture here, because the world keeps grinding us down to the nub until we forget we are even hungry or alive. But *these places are still here*. You can go to them whenever you want. You can live the life they offer. You can remove the thorn from your paw.

Attentions and Artisanality

Let's put aside for a moment the question of spirit of place. It is so important that it will return in a later chapter. Right now I want to tell you what I've found in common among the people who make connected wines.

First, they all detest the term *winemaker*. A Pfalz grower named Lingenfelder once told me, "We are not wine*makers*; we do not *make wine*. We simply prepare the environment for wine to come into being." The German-speaking vintner prefers the term *cellarmaster*. I like it too; it's humbler, more craftsmanlike.

My term *attentions* is ambiguous, I know. But it is always useful to consider a vintner in terms of this question: to what is he attending? To his skill at manipulating machines and systems? To his ability to "sculpt" a wine? To getting a couple more points for his wine than his neighbor does? To beaming with pride when you say you like his wine? To letting you see what a total hot-shot he is?

Or is he attending to the flavors that come from his land, and his sensitivity in nurturing them and letting them be? The greatest German cellarmaster of the late twentieth century, Hans-Günter Schwarz, put it as perfectly as can be said: "Every time you handle a wine you remove something that cannot be put back. The smartest thing a cellarmaster can know is the right time . . . to do nothing." The worldview of such people can be summed up as: Grow the best possible grapes and then get out of the way. And growing grapes, when you do it yourself, is of course a form of tending, of working with *life*, of subsuming yourself so as to hear what these other lives need and desire, to give of their best. For such vintners, machines are a necessary evil; their real work is done with nature. It is the difference between "Hey, check *me* out, look at *my* adorable talent," and "Come with me and I'll show you this place that I love."

You see it in the elders when (if they're lucky) their children grow up to take over the estates. I've been doing this work for most of my adult life, and in nearly every instance of generational transfer, the parents *go back into the vineyard*. It is the work that most fulfills them. They are away from sales, tanks, pumps, presses; they are back with living things. I'll never forget the Austrian vintner Engelbert Prieler, deflecting my compliments toward his daughter Silvia, who had taken control of the cellar. He wouldn't even field a question: "Oh, don't ask me, I'm just a simple farmer now. . . ." He did, however, claim all the credit for the *quality* of the wines, much to our mutual amusement—Silvia knows her dad much too well to be offended. Whatever compliment I gave, even the most innocuous, Engelbert grinned and twinkled and said, "Yes, the quality here was the result of scrupulous viticulture," or "Indeed, it goes to show what is possible when you have a genius working the vines," until finally I got it. And when I liked the next wine I turned to Dad and said, "Wow, there really was some bloody fabulous vineyard work here," and he replied, "Yes, wasn't there?"

But it's all quite sweet, you know. The older man likes being outside among the vines he has known his whole life, by himself in the fresh air. It isn't so fast out there. He can pay the kind of attention he has learned how to pay, without which one doesn't hear the earth twitter and hum. I am happy to think of these happy men.

I've seen my share of great vintages over the years, but I don't recall when I've ever seen a grower strut or preen. Most recently a fellow named Hexamer had such a remarkable vintage that he said, "I'd be lucky to have two or three more vintages like this one in my whole life." At such times I love what I see on the grower's entire visage, a thing I've seen many times when great vintages were on the table, the same thing you see on a ballplayer's face when he crosses the plate having hit the game-winning home run. He knows he has worked hard, spent his life preparing, hoping for a moment like this one. But when it comes, all he does is wonder. He's too amazed even to feel proud. He is almost embarrassed to be showered with such good fortune, as if it had nothing to do with him. *Look what happened,* he seems to say.

The pride these people feel is a craftsman's pride in work well done. When we think of "humble," we call up images of pathological self-debasement or else some mumbly "Aw, shucks," but there's another way it shows. The ego's need to insist on alpha status is calmed when one is fundamentally content, and what makes you content is to be gratefully aware that *you get to do this work.* I have never seen good wine come from an unhappy vintner. I doubt if it can. Being grateful doesn't banish the ego; it matures it. And the mature ego is reinforced when it is grounded in the natural world.

You can try to impose yourself over nature, but it leads into a blind alley and you do collateral damage to your soul. Every vintner I know is content to exist in nature as a listener who wants to hear what it asks. Few of them are mystical at all that I can see. But all of them are partners in a world where nature is as alive as they are. "The vineyard teaches me to wait, absorb nature, and understand my own boundaries," says Heidi Schröck, a vintner in Austria. There's a fellow feeling in such sentiments, a kind of friendliness. I don't think that beautiful wine can be made without it. You can make good wine, and you can damn sure make *impressive* wine, when you work from ego. Those wines always "show" well, but there's a coldness at their core. One symptom of this is the reduction of wine to a specimen to which a score is given. And this in turn is based on the idea that "perfection" is attainable—or even desirable. When someone says, "This is as good as it gets," I always want to reply, "Really? *How do you know?*" We'll revisit this topic, believe me.

Fundamental to the idea of artisanality is the appreciation of imperfection. Imperfection squares with what we observe in ourselves, our fellow humans, and all throughout nature. The natural world may be sublime, but it isn't perfect. When you make love to another person, you bring your fallibilities and flaws to hers or his. Maybe you feel fat or achy or preoccupied, or maybe you feel wonderful, but the point is that *you can't predict how you'll feel*, and you damn sure can't predict how your partner will feel, but in this collision of imperfections something valid occurs. Alternatively, you could watch porn; it's always perfect there, and you can rewind and watch your favorite parts again and again. But you are ineluctably *separate* from the images on the screen. No, it isn't perfection we need to seek; it is imperfection, because the assumption of imperfection is the thing that allows the miracle, and the swoon.

The tender attentions of the artisan are the most important prerequisite for authentic, meaningful wines, to be enjoyed by each of us imperfect beings, in our imperfect lovely world.

three

REMYSTIFYING WINE

First of all, everything is unified, everything is linked together, everything is explained by something else and in turn explains another thing. There is nothing separate, that is, nothing that can be named or described separately. In order to describe the first impressions, the first sensations, it is necessary to describe all at once. The new world with which one comes into contact has no sides, so that it is impossible to describe first one side and then the other. All of it is visible at every point. —P. D. Ouspensky

Either nature has a kind of consciousness, and therefore a purpose, or it does not. In our present state of development, there's no way to know. It's my experience that nature—whether metallic (like my car) or organic (like a plant) or neither (like the wind)—behaves differently if one relates to it as though it is conscious; many have experienced consciousness in rocks, flora, fauna and objects, but our subjective experiences are difficult to demonstrate and impossible to prove. If nature has no consciousness or purpose, I don't see how humanity can, so I choose to believe we all do. That's my sense of things. Again, impossible to prove, especially when the evidence appears to point the other way. —Michael Ventura

James Hillman and Michael Ventura published a provocative book called *We've Had 100 Years of Psychotherapy and the World's Getting Worse*. Well, we've had what seems like a hundred books purporting to "demystify" wine, and wine is more mysterious than ever. Not that the technocrat-enologist complex hasn't been furiously laboring to remove every pesky variable from wine—damn that nature!—and Lord knows we're ever more inundated with all manner of mass-produced industrial swill, but true wine is *supposed* to be complex, and if you think you know it all, well, pal, you don't know nuthin'.

Ah, but the poor hapless consumer, faced with the groaning shelves of wine bottles with gobbledygook on the labels, or the Talmudic opacity of some eight-pound document called the restaurant wine list—what can we do to help this innocent waif, terrified he'll pick the "wrong" wine? The first thing is to remind him of the nature of the risk. Let's remember, he probably has little to no idea how an automobile actually functions, and if you stuck his head under the hood, he'd think, *Hmm, why yes, that's an engine, all right,* while remaining clueless about how it makes his car move. He's getting ready to spend serious money on a machine whose operation he doesn't understand, yet we're writing books fussing over how difficult wine is? What are you out if you make a "mistake" and buy the "wrong" wine, twenty bucks in a store? This is not a major disappointment.

Underlying the wine-simplification industry is an inferiority complex. Actually, two inferiority complexes. The first belongs to the reader, who thinks he should know more about wine since apparently he can't escape it, and he hates to feel incompetent. The second belongs to wine writers, who feel themselves part of a collective failure to get Americans to drink more wine. Anything we can do, they reason, to make wine *safe* for the novice will cause him to snuggle up to wine, and this is good because we who sell wine for a living want more wine drinkers.

But what if we were talking about literature? Not enough people read, that's for sure. But they like looking at images, this we know, so let's simplify this whole literature business by making graphic books out of all those annoying *wordy* things. Once that's done, let's see if we can eliminate even *more* words, and tell the whole story with drawings. Oh, hell, let's forget about even having an object you have to hold in your hands; let's make a video of it and shove it onto a screen. I mean, it's the same story, right? Anna still throws herself in front of the train. Holden's still fussing about the stupid ducks. What's the difference?

What often underlies the desire to simplify wine, to make it more "accessible" to everyman, is perilously close to pandering: "If I kill its essence and make it incredibly simple, then will you start drinking it?" Why should we enable everyone's childish desire for things to be predictable? You want predictable, stay clear of wine. Oh, there's plenty of predictable wine made, and if you find one you like, then by all means keep drinking and enjoying it. But if you find yourself curious about wine, you have to accept that uncertainty is inextricable from the experience. Vintages vary, at least in many of the Old World's uncertain climates, and the crisp wine you liked this year could be a voluptuous wine next year. Different growers with adjacent parcels in the same vineyard will make different-tasting wine. It isn't total chaos—there are threads of consistency running through artisanal wines—but to appreciate these wines you need a tolerance for surprise.

Put it this way: Would you rather watch a ballgame as it's played, not knowing the outcome? Or would you rather cue up the DVD player and watch a tape of a game already played, maybe a great game, but one with no element of surprise?

There's very little that's inherently mystifying about wine; there's just a huge number of them, from different grapes and different places, and most of them change their taste a little each year. It's a lot of data, but it isn't integral calculus. There is, though, something that summons the *mystical* in fine wines, and this experience is available to anyone who's willing to prepare for it. It begins with being available—in other words, allowing both your attention and your emotions to respond to sensation, and to feelings of joy in the face of beauty. This is not a big deal. Say you go for a walk but you're preoccupied (that damned Blauman contract still isn't signed, and little Johnny needs braces). You see nothing of your surroundings. But then your cell phone rings, and it's Jenkins with good news: "Blauman signed!" And now your mind is liberated, and you don't just notice things, you notice *everything.* You pick up a leaf and turn it over, and the pattern on the underside is astonishing, my God, look at this, was this always here, do other people know about how amazing this is?

There is nothing esoteric or inaccessible about this state of mind. If you are aware of the world, things will come to your attention. One of them is beauty, and one of the beautiful things is wine. But wine's abilities do not stop at mere sensual beauty. Wine is able to channel multiple currents of beauty, from the pretty to the charming, from the fleeting to the logical, from the passionate to the pensive. And great wine will take you to a question and, wonderfully, deposit you there, without an answer or a map—just looking at the question.

Ambiguous? If you're sitting on a hilltop enjoying a view, you may be able to say, "This is beautiful because I can see a great distance, and the hills fold into one another in an especially comely way, and the river is perfectly situated to give depth to the scene," and that is certainly part of the truth. But beauty has a face that's turned away from the light. Think of music. Can you say *why* a certain piece of music makes you feel so intensely? Probably not. But it has happened to most of us, and we don't think ourselves weird or "new agey" when it does, because this experience, though mystical, is commonplace. It happens with wine too, but it seems outré because wine drinking itself seems the purview of the arugula munchers.

Wine may have a particular hold on this mystical faculty based on the proximity of the parts of the brain that process smells and memories. I've never had my own Proustian moment, but for me wine does something even more astounding than that. I may not suddenly recover my own memories, but a few great wines have seemed to dilate the world so that I seem to experience a *collective* memory. I might smell an old Loire valley Chenin Blanc, and it makes me think of an armoire. That's not too fanciful. But it makes me think of an armoire in a room in a French country house, and I can see the other furniture too, and the view of gardens and fields out the window, and I can almost hear the voices of the people who live in the house, and smell the body scents on the clothes hanging in my make-believe armoire.

So here is silly old me, in my imaginary room with the armoire; I hear the voices and see the fields and smell the smells, but then I sense a kind of rising; I am in the sky somehow, I see the roads linking "my" house to the other houses and then to the market village, I see the forests and the horses in the fields, and the kids playing or stealing apples, and the orchard owner running behind them swearing, and then I think, *They're not here anymore, where did they go?* And I sense an endless succession of brief lives, of people trying to work, and love, and be safe, and understand what it all means, and I am further away than ever from what it all means but there is within it all a tremendous

gravity, tenderness, and sadness for our strange species so heedless and so angelic.

Now, who knows; maybe I'm recovering an embedded memory of some inconsequential scene in Turgenev I read thirty
years ago. Or maybe it's a manifestation of wine's strange ability
to arouse the imagination. This is the "mystical" facet of wine,
and I don't think we should apologize for it or be embarrassed
about it or seek to quash it. I think we need not to demystify
wine, but to *remystify* it!

I return to the wine in my glass. What I just described took
place in a second or two. I haven't figured out how to summon it,
but I try to be there when it summons me. It means well by me.

I work with a grower named Martin Nigl, who makes especially ethereal wines, the kinds of wines that pose questions we
never thought to ask: How far can refinement be taken? What
do we find there? Clarity reveals flavor, as we know, but what
is on the far side of clear flavor? I also wonder how wines like
Nigl's make me feel, because they don't generate a volume of
emotional affect. They are too searching. Perhaps what they
generate most is curiosity. If I haven't imagined that wine can
offer such pure refinement, what else haven't I imagined?

I think that wines like Nigl's can inculcate an appreciation of
detail and design. They're like dew-covered webs you see in the
morning, when you pause to appreciate the craft of the weaver,
all curled into a tiny nugget, waiting for the sun to strike her.
Or hoarfrost on your windows some winter morning, as you
study the intricacy of the crystals. When I was a little guy I had
a microscope, just a little one but more than a toy, and I loved
to look at my slides. And now flavors are under a microscope,
showing all the worlds within worlds, all below our vision.

This is not to say that Nigl's wines leave all sensual life

behind; far from it. They are feasts for the senses, but theirs is an esoteric cuisine that will feed the hungers you know, and the ones you're unaware of. But you have to be available for this experience, and to listen in a different way. It won't leave you happier, but it does leave you wondering, because there is *more* of you on the other side. And you don't need to contrive some great vast rapture in order to know this moment. It can live, and lives quite easily, in a single sip of wine.

So why not just relax with wine? Don't worry about what you know or don't know. Don't even worry about what you're "supposed" (according to the likes of me) to feel. Just daydream and release your imagination. Believe me, it's more fun than trying to grab a wine, to nail the poor bastard, to dissect it in order to show how cool your palate is. What a pitiable waste! It's like ignoring a rainbow so you can balance your checkbook.

Bear in mind, the cultivation of the mystic isn't only a pursuit of refined experience—in fact, it isn't any sort of *pursuit* at all. The mystic also reveals itself by presenting and encouraging intuition and metaphor. Each of these can come to you if you're relaxed. I recall sitting in a tasting room at the estate of Carl Loewen (from whom we heard in chapter 2) and noticing that I always heard blackbirds when I tasted there. I found a charming connection between the companionship of the songbird and the unassuming but lovely wine. This is probably because Carl's tasting room is just inside his garden, and there's always a blackbird trilling away in the background. Nature does enjoy showcasing her metaphors! But I delight in the juxtaposition of the wine in my glass with the whistling and warbling outside. Here's this little blackbird singing its tiny lungs out, all that energy and melody coming from such a tiny, delicate body, and in the glass there's a wine with 8 percent alcohol, all that energy and melody coming from such a tiny, delicate body. I wonder what the metaphor would be if you were tasting, hmm, in Australia. Some huge malevolent beast bellowing outside in the dust.

If you see the world sacramentally—apart from whatever religious affiliation you may have, or even if you have none at all—you find you have learned to assume that things are connected. Austrian grower Michael Moosbrugger has leased a venerable monastic estate called Schloss Gobelsburg. The land was superb, but the current generation of monks wanted help in modernizing the property and aligning the wines with prevailing standards of quality.

Michael went about upgrading the wines squarely within the context of modern quality-oriented winemaking, and his wines quickly became excellent, even great, as these things are currently understood and evaluated by the critical establishment. Within a few years he had accomplished his goal, only to learn that his true goal lay elsewhere, somewhere both further on and deeper inside.

It started when he tasted through the estate's cellar of old vintages. The wines were different, less modern; the current wines seemed almost sterile in contrast to these mossy old things. And Michael wondered, What guided the old wines? Did those old monks simply lack the know-how of modern cellarmasters? Or was something else at work? The monks kept detailed records. It was easy to see what they did with their wines. But all this did was to ignite a deeper curiosity. What if he went *very* far back, to the period between the end of the Franco-Prussian War and the start of World War I? What did those monks know that we have forgotten?

It is so easy to make this sentimental and trivial. "Return to the wisdom of the monks" is guaranteed to make my eyes glaze over. It is not what I mean. Michael set about to produce a wine—eventually, two wines—as they would have been made almost one hundred years ago. He didn't intend them as an "homage," and certainly not as a pastiche. He couldn't be sure how the wines would be. He only sought to *know*.

"If you consider the span of time between the Romans and the nineteenth century, a Roman who would have been catapulted forward in time would not have been surprised by what he saw," Michael says. "But in the last hundred years, everything has changed, and our own mentalities have changed also. These days we seek to preserve primary fruit as much as possible, and the ways we do it are to ferment at lower temperatures and not to agitate the wine. But until very recently none of this was technologically possible. In those days the guiding idea was that a wine was *schooled*, like a child is schooled—the French call it *élevage*—until it reached a stage in its development when it was ready to drink. And then it was bottled."

How did they know? I asked. "They knew by taste, and also by the extent to which the wine attained the Ideal they had for it." It sounds like a kind of *ripening*, I said. "Yes, exactly; the wine said when it was ready, when it reached the development they'd guided it toward."

Therefore Michael had gone back to a time when oxygen wasn't feared in winemaking. Indeed, it couldn't be avoided, so you adapted to it. You understood wine as a beverage *dependent* on oxygen to create the nongrape flavors by which it was *wine* and not just fermented grape juice. In place of the modern trend for whole-cluster pressing (and the crystalline texture it creates), Michael crushed and pressed his grapes on their skins; he fermented the juice without clarifying it (the old ones used to say he "fermented with all the *schmutz* and bacon"); he eschewed temperature control; he put the wine in old casks and racked it often to *encourage* secondary flavors, the nongrape flavors we call "vinosity," all to replicate this old vinous dialect, which was almost extinct.

What moves me most, apart from the quality of these wines, is what I interpret as Michael's search for *soul*. I imagine we all suspect that soul is, or can be, crowded out by technology, if only because it is so tempting to surrender to the machine's ease, its sterile exactitude, that which we once knew in our fingertips. Each time you flick a switch on a machine you erect a membrane between yourself and your wine. Sometimes this is a necessary evil. I don't want to endorse any kind of feel-good nostalgia. But I like to make meatballs, and while I could easily do the mixture in a food processor, I prefer doing it with my hands because I like that my hands know when it's ready. So I can see how a vintner could be prone to ennui if he merely flicked the switch and the machine did the rest.

I'm not making any sort of Luddite case for pretechnological wines, nor do I suppose they have a nostalgic value. I only share Michael's fascination with how it must have been for the people who made wines as best they could in those times, and created a set of values predicated on what was, and was not, possible. I share Michael's intuition that something of soul, something we may have misplaced, is there to be found. I share that hunger, and I know the rare thing that feeds it. When intuition is all you have, you nurture intuition! And intuition isn't quantifiable, and whatever we can't quantify slips between the threads of what we call understanding. And what we don't understand we call mystic, with mistrust and derision.

There's a lot we can understand about wine, and among those things there's nothing more salient than understanding the *limits* to understanding. Wine is bigger than us, and this is perfect, it is why we spend our lives in love with it; and if this is mystifying, then please, *bring it on*.

four

THE THREE HUMORS

O ver the course of three decades of drinking wine, I began
to realize which among its enticements were most important. This has to happen empirically; you can't go in with
assumptions already formed. You have to learn to recognize the
difference between what you think you value and what you actually do. For me the things that matter become apparent when I
see which topics I get into arguments about. I am not by nature
a quarrelsome fella; I believe in sweet reason. But that doesn't
preclude passion, so here are the facets of wine with which I'm
most absorbed, and which I'm most convinced are central to
understanding and appreciating wine, and its place in a rich and
juicy life.

I call them the three humors, but they can just as easily be
called the three cruxes. They imbue my every thought and feeling about wine. Yet I barely ever actually *do* think about them
discretely (I spend most of my time thinking about baseball, sex,
and guitar solos . . . ever the rock-star wanna-be) because I'd be
paralyzed with self-consciousness. Nonetheless I find myself

asserting and defending precisely these three values when I talk
or write about wine.

- One, wine should express an emergence from its particular
  origin.
- Two, in considering this and other abstract values, we
  should never forget to respond spontaneously to wine's
  sensual value. Laugh when you're tickled, please!
- Three, we should be aware that wine takes us to the edge of
  language, and sometimes to the edge of what we can know.
  I'm instinctively sure that this is centrally important—not
  only to our lives as wine drinkers, but to our entire lives.

These three "humors" could be called the spatial, the sensual, and the spiritual. Their borders are porous: each inheres in
the others, and all of them permeate everything we experience
in wine.

The First Humor: Specificity

Why should wines taste of their origin? The question is not
rhetorical. Wines should indicate their specific origins in flavorsome ways because, in part, many of us *want* them to. But we are
a great mess of different temperaments, and some people claim
that only sensual pleasure is important, no matter how it might
be contrived. Sensual pleasure is crucially important, and sometimes it's the right place to stop, but not always. Some people
seem uneasy with the notion that wine could *signify* something.
I'm not here to throw psychobabble at their motives—tempting
though that is—but rather to try to answer the question inher-

ent in their challenge. I am claiming that the flavor of origin *matters*, and it's reasonable to be asked why.

In the not-very-distant past there were lots of people who said that terroir—which for my current purpose I'm defining as the particular flavor from a particular place, based first on soil— is a lot of meretricious mumbo-jumbo. Doesn't exist, except as a romantic notion cherished by those who drink with extended pinkies. Well, that idea didn't seem to gain much traction. Many New World vintners who were among the most vocal opponents of terroir as a core factor in flavor have since signed on, or would like you to think they have. Perhaps they are evolving, perhaps it's a matter of can't-lick-'em-join-'em, or perhaps it's a wee bit cynical. . . .

There are wine drinkers whose vector is hedonistic, and in many cases they're proudly pragmatic. Wine, in their view, is a thing that can be engineered to press certain pleasure buttons. These pragmatic hedonists eventually (and grudgingly) yielded the point of terroir when they could no longer reasonably deny it. But even as they mumbled, *Well, yes, it does seem to exist, I guess*, they claimed (in very loud voices now) that *it didn't matter.* Terroir might well be real, they said, but if it isn't blatant enough to nail reliably in a blind tasting, then how important could it really be? I'll tell you.

That an effect is subtle doesn't make it unimportant. Significance is not established or validated by obviousness. If for argument's sake I grant the point that terroir shows only in delicate ways, how does that make it any less significant? Yet this is not the crucial issue at hand. To identify that issue I'm going to proceed elliptically. My argument is more holistic than linear, though *holistic* does not connote *illogical*, but only asks for a tolerance for fluid logic—a hard proposition for the pragmatic hedonist. Remember, I'm asking, Why does this all matter? And here's what I'd say.

Some years ago I was a panelist at a sustainable-agriculture conference. Our topic was spirit of place, and toward the end of the discussion a Native American woman to my left said something I have never forgotten. "The salmon do not only return to the stream to spawn," she said. "They also return to respond to the prayers and hopes of the people who love them."

I think that's a lovely thing to say—to believe—and quoted it in one of my sales catalogs. I also thought the statement was innocuous enough to be accepted at least as a bit of poetry. So I was taken aback when a reader called it "pretentious new-age bullshit." I had to ask why anyone could be so enraged by what struck me as a commonplace enough statement from someone who sees the world sacramentally. I recognize there are sensibilities other than mine, more logical and prosaic. Yet with all respect, most thoughts along the "mystical" continuum can be rephrased in linear equations—if one insists.

No, the salmon aren't actually thinking, *Let's hurry back to the river, guys, 'cause the Indians are waiting for us.* No one means to say that. There is, though, among certain people (and peoples) an assumption of immersion in nature that is essentially different from the subject-object relationship most of us presume. I am not *apart* from nature, I am *a part* of it, as it is of me, and everything I see tells me that all living things are unified. The idea of the salmon "responding" may be poetic, but the notion of life's basic interconnectedness is entirely reasonable. That doesn't mean I don't swat as many flies as the next guy, but it's hardly mystical to recognize that each of our discrete lives is part of a general life force. If someone wants to believe the spirits or gods inhabit the salmon too, I find it less objectionable than to assume that we humans have perfect knowledge of where the gods do and do not live!

Life takes many forms, as of course we know. But how often do we actually pause to consider how lucky we are that people look different from one another? I wonder how it would be if we could be engineered to look like some standardized ideal of beauty. Everyone would be attractive, or "attractive," and we'd all look the same. I wonder if someone would yearn for the good old days when people were idiosyncratic and asymmetrical and sometimes not all that gorgeous—but always unique and recognizable, *because of where they came from.* I think it's better—not relatively better, but truly inherently better—when wine shows us its origin. Because if *it* has an origin, then *so do we;* so does every true thing. Wine that expresses its identity reinforces the value of identity. That's part of why it matters, but not all.

Although I assume there is unity among all living things, I don't imagine that this is pretty, and sometimes it's damned inconvenient. But I can't find reason to believe otherwise. Thus it isn't much of a stretch to infer spirit into places, based on the varieties of lives to be found there. Qualities of light, of vegetation, of fauna and people, and of the things people do—what they grow, how they celebrate, how much their ears stick out: all of it. Wine is one of the ways a place conveys its spirit to us. And this matters because we *are* in fact connected—even if we deny it, and even if we aren't aware—and if we claim that wine is important in our lives, then wine must also be bound into and among the filaments that connect us to all things. Wines that are made for commercial purposes and exist merely as products have to take their place alongside all such commodities: soda, breakfast cereal, vacuum-cleaner bags. They can be enjoyable and useful, but they don't matter. They don't matter because they don't *live*. They don't live because they don't come from a recognizable place.

Spirit of place is a concept that's like really good soap; it's lovely, it feels good when it touches you, and it's slippery as hell. It isn't announced with billboards, you know. SPIRIT OF PLACE, FIVE MILES AHEAD; BEAR RIGHT TO ACCESS. Not like that. Nor is it necessarily beautiful. The northern section of the New Jersey Turnpike is *full* of spirit of place, repugnant though it may be. I think spirit of place comes at the moment of ignition between your soul and that place, and a condition of that union is that you don't notice it happening. It is an inference, as all soul things are.

I'll give an example. In Champagne there is a road I like, down an alley of fine old elms leading to the Marne at Damery: France at its most sylvan and tranquil. At first I thought it odd that such a serene landscape should yield such a vivacious wine. But then I realized that the vivacity of Champagne is not only the voice of the landscape, but of the crisp nights in early September and the cool days in June and the wan northern sun that seldom seems to roast. And the still wines of Champagne are rarely vivid in the way young Riesling or Muscat can be. They are pastel, aquarelle, restrained, gauzy. Add bubbles and they get frisky, but they aren't born that way.

Champagne grower Didier Gimonnet told me that a wine writer had been pestering him to bottle a separate cuvée of superrich wine from an eighty-plus-year-old vineyard he owns.

"I'll never do it," he insists, "because the wine would be too powerful." *But isn't that the point?* I thought. Isn't that what wine's supposed to do in our skewered age? Density, opacity, power, flavor that can break bricks with its head! No, said Gimonnet: "I think Champagne needs a certain transparency in order to be elegant." And then it came to me.

Here was the aesthetic to correspond to the gentle Champenois landscape. A *pays* of low hills, forested summits, and plain, sleepy villages isn't destined to produce powerful wines. We might demand them, but we've become so besotted by our demand for impact that we're forgetting how to discern *beauty*. And who among us ever tilts a listening ear to hear the hum of the land?

Is that, too, insignificant? One reason the Old World calls to us is that these lands *do* hum, in a subterranean vibration you feel in your bones, especially if you are an American unaccustomed to the experience. The hum existed for centuries before you got here. It isn't meant for you to fathom. It is mysterious, and you are temporary, but it connects you to vast currents of generations and time. And you are tickled by a sense of meaning you can't quite touch.

It is rarely the same for Americans. Each of us is the crown of creation. We invented humanity. Nothing happened before us, or in any case nothing worth remembering. Memory is nothing but a burden anyway. We turn to the world like a playground bully looking to pick a fight. "Whaddaya got *today* to amuse me, pal? How ya gonna impress me? How many *points* will this day be worth?" Oh, maybe our little slice of earth rumbles with its own hum, but if so then few Americans want to know how to hear it, and most are suspicious of the value of listening at all. For me and my countrymen the taste of place is an anchoring we don't know how badly we need.

Does spirit of place reside integrally within a place, or do we read it in? The answer is *yes*. We are a part of all we experience, and if we glean the presence of spirit of place, then it's there in part *because* we glean it—we bring it to consciousness, one might say. I want to emphasize that point. The soul records, but does not transcribe. Because we are part of nature, what happens to us also happens *in nature*. This is self-evident. From this point one ventures forth according to one's curiosity and temperament. I prefer to believe that spirit of place registers with us because *nature wants it to*, because everything that happens in nature is part of a—dangerous word coming up—design. Not the "design" co-opted by the religious right seeking to challenge Darwin, but an ordering of existence and experience that we humans discern, which is also part of the self-same design.

Whether this design has purpose can be reduced to our sense of faith or just to intellectual entertainment. If I choose to believe there is no purpose, then there's nothing left to think about, it's all random and senseless, and let's see what's on TV. Assuming that things aren't mere chance is, at the very least, an invitation to *keep thinking*.

How do we know when wine is expressing spirit of place? This is actually easier than it might appear. Tangibly, a wine expresses its origin when it *flourishes* and tells us it is happy. It says, "Here is where I'm at home," and I believe we taste flourishing when a grape variety speaks with remarkable articulation, complexity, and harmony in its wines. Generations of winegrowers had centuries of trial and error to learn which grapes made the best wine on their land, but one taste and *we* know immediately. And the noblest grapes are persnickety about which places they call home. Grapes grow mute when planted in foreign soil. Riesling planted in warmer climates than it likes, or on over-rich soils, gives a blatantly fruit-salady wine that most people correctly reject as dull or cloying. Has Chenin Blanc ever made great wine outside of Anjou and Touraine? Nebbiolo seems not to flourish outside Piemonte. I'd even argue that Chardonnay is strictly at home in Chablis (and possibly also in Champagne), since this seems the only terroir where it is inherently interesting and can manage without the pancake makeup of oak or other manipulations.

When a vine is at home, it settles in and starts to transmit. We "hear" those transmissions as flavors. A naturally articulate grape like Riesling sends clear messages of the soil, a panoply of nuances of fruits, flowers, and stones, flavors that are consistent, specific, and repeated year after year, varied only by the weather in which that year's grapes ripened. Vintners know those flavors in their bones. They don't have to wait for the wine in order to detect them; they can taste them in the must. They can taste them in the *grapes*. You wouldn't have to sermonize to these people about spirit of place. They are steeped in that spirit as a condition of life. Indeed, their inchoate assumption that a place contains spirit is *part* of that spirit.

An invitation is implied in spirit of place. When someone like Mosel grower Willi Schaefer goes about his work, he does so with certainty that the Domprobst vineyard will taste one way and the Himmelreich another. He doesn't think about it abstractly—he's too close in—but if you asked him, he'd say he likes that the earth expresses itself in *various* ways. He is also aware of his place in a continuum of generations who have worked the land, land that existed before him and will exist when he's gone, and which has always given the same flavors in the same ways. Willi takes his place within nature and cares for his vines and soils; he would never dream he had *dominion* over nature, or that a vineyard was merely a production-unit to be bent to his will. Unique flavors come into his wine because they are *already there* and he gets out of the way. Why would he do otherwise?

When he tastes his wines, he is fascinated with each unique nuance of identity, and we can likewise be fascinated when we drink his wines, linked together in mutual fascination, he to his land and we to him. And so we are also linked to his land. None of this is "mystical"! Wines of distinctiveness will ground us in a nexus of meaning. Humility before nature is meaningful. Connection to our fellow folks is meaningful. Connection to places we don't otherwise know is meaningful because it stimulates dreams and longing, of faraway places and of the lovely multiplicity of things.

But spirit of place doesn't dwell only in the details. The Mosel, that limpid little river, flows through a gorge it has created amid almost impossibly steep mountainsides. Its people are conservative, and they approach the sweaty work on the steep slopes with humility and good cheer. They are—global warming notwithstanding—northerly people, accustomed to a bracing and taut way of life. Is it an accident that their wines are also bracing and taut? Insist that it's pure coincidence, and I'll wager you were never there. If you were there and you still don't see it, Customs must have confiscated your imagination.

We need wines that tell us in no uncertain terms, "I hail from *this* place and this alone, not from any other, for only here am I at home." Such wines transport us to those places. If we are already there, they cement the reality of our being there. We need to know where we are. If we do not, we are *lost*.

I don't have time to waste on processed wines that taste as if they could have come from anywhere, because in fact they come from nowhere and have no place to take me. We crave spirit of place because of our own need to be located, which reassures us that we belong in the universe. We want our bearings. We want to know where home is. We can deny or ignore this longing, but it will scrape away at us relentlessly while we wonder why we feel so homesick, why we never feel whole.

Or we can claim this world of places. We can claim the love that lives in hills and vines, in trees and birds and smells, in buildings and ovens and human eyes, of everything in our world that makes itself at home and calls on us to do the same. The value of wine, beyond the sensual joy it gives us, lies in what it shows us—not only its own hills and rivers, but the road home.

The Second Humor: Fun, and Why It Runs from Us

I had two unsettling anniversaries in 2008: thirty years of drinking wine seriously, and twenty-five years in the wine business. And as these dates approached, I began to wonder whether the longer we all drink wine, the less fun we have with it.

I don't think this is necessarily because we grow jaded, but rather because of the kinds of wines we select for ourselves: *earnest* wines, emblems of a "serious" or "passionate" approach, wines that compel our full attention. A metaphor for this phenomenon is the creature called the restaurant wine list, which, if you're ordering for the table, means that for minutes on end—often many, many minutes on end—you are ignoring your guests. These tomes insist that we pay heed: *it's all about the wine*, you see.

Many wine professionals were wine hobbyists to start out, and we head-butted our way into the business because it seemed like fun to make money doing what we were doing anyway: obsessing about wine. In my early days there was no difference between the "work" I did and the place of wine in my private life. For me it was kind of sweet, but for those around me it must have seemed that the business was open 24/7.

A few years ago I started to see the roads diverge. When I drank wine at home—drank, not tasted or "appraised" or evaluated from any professional standpoint—I wanted something *recreational*, ideally something different from "work" wines. At least, I wished for a wine that would be wholly satisfying but not necessarily demanding. What kinds of wines would these be? Did my portfolio already contain them, my work encompass them? If not, *why not?* And what did this all say about the kinds of wines I actually, spontaneously, sensually found *yummy?*

I know full well that wine can be important, that it can be an embodiment of culture, that it can be a messenger of meaning, a portal into the mystery. But if wine must always be solemnly Important, then life gets pretty dour. Here are some other things wine can be.

It was a pretty midday in early May when I visited Jamek in Austria's Wachau. Along with the winery there is a venerable restaurant that should have a high place as a culinary

UNESCO heritage site, and I was asked if I wanted to sit and taste outdoors—"It's the first day we've set up the tables in the garden." And so I did. I was alone, with the superattentiveness one has at table alone. At Jamek you always taste somewhere in the restaurant, as if to emphasize the connections among wine, food, regionality. The garden slowly filled with people pausing to enjoy their lives on a soft spring day among the flowers and the blackbirds and the trees. Some brought their dogs, who lay cooperatively under the table as well-behaved Eurodogs do. I watched food and wine being served and wondered, *What role does wine play here? To what does it pertain?* Do wine professionals ever think about how wine fits into other aspects of our lives, or is it just wine qua wine for us?

It is something to see wine drunk without fuss in a spring garden as the world twitters and blossoms and people eat their salads and schnitzels and pike perch. However much *we* may obsess, wine itself goes about its genial business of washing down people's meals and gracing their lives for an hour.

At the end of one year's tasting tour of Austria, entailing much concentration and many days of writing tasting notes, I took myself off to the Alps for a couple of days to clear my head. At times the need to write tasting notes is intrusive, like pausing to describe the giddy ecstatic running of a dog for whom you've just thrown a stick. The grinning beast lopes back to you with a big ol' drool-covered stick in his slobbery maw, and he's looking at you as if every scintilla of his happiness depends on your throwing that stick again, and what are you doing? You're writing! Put down the pen and throw the damn stick, man!

My friends at Jamek had given me a bottle of a Muskateller they saw I enjoyed. Once in the mountains, I spent the afternoon hiking, enjoying my solitude and blissful not to have to think. I ate a simple dinner and washed it down with a carafe of pretty dubious Blaufränkisch. Up in my room again, the sun was setting and the peaks were napped in that late-day amber, and I had my bottle of Muscat. So I went down and asked for a wineglass. I took it upstairs, sat on my little balcony, and glugged a wine that seemed to encapsulate the keen mountain air. Eventually I jettisoned the glass and just drank from the bottle. Those moments were perfect: the wine was content not to occupy my whole attention, but rather just to keep me company.

It can grow tedious, you know, to encounter a "great" wine that spends the whole evening talking about itself. Obviously the truly great wine both compels and warrants all the attention one is willing to give it, but for every sublime and articulate wine there are a few dozen chatterboxes and bores.

We risk squandering the capacity to enjoy that which is simple because we seemingly need to insist that it be *merely* simple, or that simple isn't good enough for us. Great, complex wines are wonderful, enthralling, life-affirming, soul-stirring, but it's worth asking whether they are *relaxing*. Good, simple wines are. Good, simple wines speak to our spirit of play and ease and repose, exactly because they don't demand our exclusive attention.

One summer I met a friend in San Francisco and we played hooky and took a picnic up to the cliffs of the Marin headlands, where we sat watching pelicans dive into the Pacific. We had a bottle of Bardolino rosé, but no glasses. No matter! That bottle emptied pronto. My companion was a "wine friend," but we spoke not a word about that Bardolino. Yet we were limbically united in the almost animal pleasure each of us took in it.

What has to happen in such moments? The wine has to be good enough that you can trust it without having to think about it. There's a tiny second of ignition—yup, it's good—and then you return to your life. Great wine would be too intrusive, but a wholly *good* wine is ideal.

I've taken customers with me to Austria from time to time. One has to be careful how to stage these trips. You can't front-load too many serious estates when people are still tired and jet-lagged. So on the second day of one such trip I took the group to Hans Setzer and Erich Berger, and taught myself a lesson in the process. Both of these estates make wines of charm. That doesn't preclude significance as we might measure it, but it refers to a different aesthetic. I suddenly found myself inside a kind of spell: "These wines, whatever else they might be, are *delicious*," it said.

Delicious. Who uses that word to talk about wine anymore? A hamburger might be delicious, but a Gigondas? And what makes a wine delicious? Can we isolate its elements? Should we even try?

I believe we should try—not to kill it by dissection, but rather to contemplate the value that such deliciousness deserves, and seldom receives. And I would argue that the first element of deliciousness is *charm*.

Of all the aesthetic virtues, charm is perhaps the most imperiled. We have a little carousel at our county's regional park, and I like to pause there during a long walk and watch the little kids whirl around on the painted horses. One week I noticed they'd given up the usual calliope music in favor of—god help me—disco. And it was just so damn *wrong*, all these three- and four-year-olds riding along to "I Will Survive." Is calliope music supposed to be too goofy or unhip or some stupid thing?

Charm is among the highest virtues. In people it denotes an effort of behavior whereby you feel appreciated and cared for. In wine or music it creates a response of palpable delight. I find this feeling more pleasant than many other feelings that have greater *prestige.* Of course, there's a place in me for being knocked out, blown away, stunned, impressed, but none of these is as exquisitely joyful as feeling charmed. Also, charm is a flexible virtue, able to exist in big wines, medium wines, or little wines. I prize this quality of charm because it seems less reducible to recipe. Any grower of unexceptional talent can make intense wine, but to craft charming wines is less a matter of formula than of intuition and attending to myriad tiny details, knowing all the while that your wine won't be the biggest, boldest, or loudest wine on the table. Instead it will insinuate, will crawl inside a certain temperament and sing its lyric song, and this is the pleasure for which we live.

Do I perhaps overstate the case? Charm isn't all that impossible; just ferment with aroma yeasts at cold temperatures to get those sweet banana aromas and leave a little residual sugar behind, maybe throw a little Muscat into the Veltliner and *presto*, there's your charm. Not so. Lovers of true charm are not seduced by the specious or formulaic. Charm asks the grower to pay heed to *texture* and, even harder, to attend to flavor in a different way: not how much of it there is, but how *pleasing* it is.

The mere affectation of charm is indeed abhorrent, and such phonies are all too easy to spot. The awareness of being seduced usually precludes the seduction! The truly seductive wine ignites a spontaneous and irresistible delight, a flush of animal pleasure at its sheer deliciousness.

At this point I'll pause to consider how I've come to worry at this possibly self-evident point. As a wine pro, I spend a great deal of time assessing wine. Does it make the cut? Is it worthy? Further, I spend a great deal of time describing wine, which often involves a kind of vivisection of its components. None of this is exceptional; professionals *work with* wine, after all. But I fear we all, pros and amateurs alike, are in danger of working *at* wine. The blatant example of this melancholy activity is the point score. I'll reserve my dudgeon at that all-too-easy target for a later chapter, except to point out an inherent limitation in all scoring systems: they cannot speak to how wine is used, but only to how it is "judged."

And at the end of a day working with wine, by evening I want a wine with which I can relax, a delicious, companionable wine. All of us in the trade know—or ought to know—that the most successful wine isn't always the one with the highest score, it is the one the tasters reach for to drink after the tasting. "The best bottle is the first one emptied," is a wise proverb.

My friend Erich Berger's wines are wines of *humor* in the classical sense, graceful and pleasurable, gregarious and celebratory. Please consider: often, when we drink a wine for "celebration," we forget what we're actually celebrating and end up celebrating the wine. Be honest, now, you know it's true! But whatever it is—your novel got published, you have an anniversary, your biopsy came back negative, your computer is fixed, you finally got laid—don't you actually need a wine that won't draw attention away from the reason you popped it in the first place? If you want to drink a great wine, or Great Wine, then celebrate *that*. Otherwise, drink a wine in which the spirit of celebration lives.

If we reorient the way we think of wine to favor wines of usefulness and companionability, interesting things happen. Wine draws closer to us. It becomes our partner in a dynamic relationship. And as we consider which wines we want in our cellars or in our lives, we find our thinking becomes more ecumenical. We appreciate wines in broader echelons of "stature." We stop insisting, and start accepting. We no longer see from the top down, grasping for the "best" without reference to the rest of our lives. We start to think about what we eat, *how we live;* which wines we drink at what times of year, whom we drink with: in short, we think of wine as we actually use it. And we let it take its natural place as a helpful being who keeps us company and eases our ways.

To know what you *really* like, look at what you're always buying more of. Speaking again of Austria, I am certain her best wines are her great Rieslings. But I'm just as certain her Grüner Veltliners are more useful to me, since I'm always reaching for them and constantly running out. Strict evaluation of wine certainly has its place, and great wine has a very noble place in our souls; but I suspect we are all too greedy for exalted experience. I like Anaïs Nin's quote "Beware of the esoteric pleasures; they will blunt your appreciation of the ordinary ones." Our craving to have our worlds rocked is a filter that excludes the very experience we so urgently clamor for. Great wine will come to you if you're calm enough to let it. And in that calm you will find a renewed (and renewable) joy in wines of loveliness, goodness, and charm.

So we've considered the value of located wines as a marker

of authenticity and meaning, and we've considered wine as an agent of fun and delight. What is left is to look at wine's strangest ability: to channel the inexplicable. And so we arrive at the frontiers of what can be said, and it's time to go exploring. Who, what lives here, and what oxygen is here to breathe?

The Third Humor: Ease with the Unknowable

We begin with a strange and unsettling thing that happened in Washington, D.C., in January 2007. The story (by the wonderful Gene Weingarten) was published in early April in the *Washington Post*, on a day when we awoke to a tracing of snow on the newly unfurled leaves.

It seems the great violinist Joshua Bell agreed to play as a busker during morning rush hour in a D.C. Metro station, just to see whether passersby would notice the presence of the extraordinary. It won't surprise you to learn that almost no one stopped to hear Bell's performance, and that many who did were actually annoyed by what they perceived as an intrusion. Yes, of course, the deck was stacked. Obviously the lives we live are all stupefying to some degree, especially when we're shooting robotically through space on our way to work, latte in hand, iPod bud in ear. We cannot reasonably accuse those heedless commuters of being (in Anne Lamott's lovely phrase) worthless philistine scum. They're merely busy drones who've accepted that much of their lives—*our* lives—will be lived on autopilot. But why am I telling you this?

This book considers a commodity that none of us needs. We can live without wine. We might not want to, but we can. Yet we care about wine in many and varied ways. At the very least it gives us sensual pleasure. Others become cerebrally intrigued by its multiplicity. Still others are more serious about wine's role in culture and history. And some of us, when we experience a wine of great beauty, are compelled to speculate on the meanings of the aesthetic experience. And we feel the curiously powerful emotion that beauty evokes. Wine is singular in this respect. Beautiful flavor can be found and appreciated in food, of course, but there is appetite involved. We seldom drink wine because we are thirsty.

I am concerned with the ways we form our relationships with beauty. Some of us don't form them. I'm also curious to know how we live when there is, by circumstance or design, a paucity of beauty in our lives.

I suspect we are all more thirsty for beauty than some of us know, or would admit. What differs is our *awareness* of the need. Temperament plays its usual role, and I suspect I am especially sensitive, not because I'm a superior person, but just because I am made that way. If you are made differently, I'll be the last guy to try to force you to fake beauty orgasms to demonstrate your sensitivity. But I believe in a universal thirst for beauty, which gets ground out of us by the sedative effect of the everyday.

I am also convinced of this: no matter how much we have or have not cherished beauty in our lives, at some point we'll regret that it wasn't more.

Wine, for me, has always been an unusually pure bringer of beauty. It is something akin to music in that respect, that is, it moves us without recourse to narrative and without stirring our empathies. In that sense it is perhaps even more pure than music, which is often contrived to produce certain emotions.

Wine is music in the form of water. Since it is such an unspoiled conveyor of beauty, I respect it in a very particular way, and I feel it needs protecting. It's way too easy to stamp wine into the ground by manipulating it in the cellar and obsessing over it in the parlor. Not too many things convey beauty to us in a form as pure as wine's.

However, a life in pursuit of beauty is vulnerable to a certain neurosis, and it can quickly grow merely precious. Groping for beauty is a good way to send it packing. Insisting that all wines must be measured by how skillfully they wiggle your beauty knob or how quickly they open your tear ducts is more than tiresome. Some wine is exceptionally vivid, and demands attention, and most of the time I am gratefully and respectfully willing to give it. Other times I want to be left in peace. There are stunningly compelling wines and there are "let me keep you company" wines, and we need them both.

And once in a great while, there are wines like those of the great Nahe vintner Helmut Dönnhoff, which simply play for you like Joshua Bell busking in the subway; they open a door but do not tap you on the shoulder—they just open the door. If you are *awake* to possibility, you'll notice the portal, and if you're curious, you will wonder where it leads.

But here, a small digression. These ways are serpentine and mossy. . . .

Like most lovers of German wine, I love Auslese, the not-quite-dessert wine that begins to show a grape's ripe essence. I buy more of it than I drink. It piles up in the cellar, and at such times it is useful to have thirsty friends and a lot of cheese—both of which I gathered together a little before Christmas one year, to drink a whole slew of mature Auslese and chow down with suitable nibbles.

The wines were very fine, all of them kinetic and articulate, some of them exciting and gripping. Then I opened a Dönnhoff, the 1990 Niederhäuser Hermannshöhle Auslese. The game was, we (or rather, *they*) tasted the first sip blind, not to guess the wine but simply to receive its signal without the noise of identity. As this wine was poured, I watched a kind of spell settle over my friends. I hadn't planned it, and I didn't suppose the wine was any better than the wines around it. But the chatter died down, and people went from witty and sociable to pensive and meditative.

What in a wine can bring about this rare and strangely truthful quality of evanescence? This strikes me as a vital question. When a wine is this searching, probing, it seems to offer something that is found no other way.

One gropes to find words. There is a saying that we should be suspicious of things for which no words exist, and although I imagine this to be true, it can't be the whole truth. Words may not exist, but *something* does. There's a drawing among the many aching works of Käthe Kollwitz called *Prisoners Listening to Music*. In it we see the wretched trying to endure the divine. We suppose that beauty has been banished from their lives. And here it is, restored; their faces are afraid and hesitant and wondering, as they see perhaps for the first time the tiny cloisters that live inside each of them, and each of us.

There are wines that convey these moments. There are wines that express without asserting, wines that show the little penumbra between joy and serenity, between brilliance and luminosity. I have tasted them, as I hope you have. Such wines are sometimes a little unnerving because they resist being grasped and they don't make statements. It also seems impossible to contrive them. And this quality confounds a certain kind of drinker who likes to vivisect how a "well-made" wine is constructed.

Recently I had an absolutely marvelous wine from the Nahe's Schlossgut Diel; it was the 2006 Goldloch "Grosses Gewächs," and it is admirable in every way. There's a lusty vein of minerality and all the baroque fruit of great Goldloch; the wine is superbly balanced, delicious, and sophisticated. It demonstrates care and intelligence, and gives a tasty joy. Yet it is entirely *tangible*, and all of its delightful facets are readily discernible.

A few evenings later I had a 2005 Steiner Hund Riesling from Austria's Nikolaihof and was once again thrust into something irreducible. Sure, I could have written a tasting note and broken it down, but there was something elusive here. Where the Diel was expressive, this wine was serene. Where the Diel was complex and delicious, this wine was exquisite and mysterious. Where the Diel was a glorious fanfare of flavor, the Nikolaihof was a lullaby. May I go further and risk looking silly? Where the Diel was giddy with its own beauty, the Nikolaihof was content with its own calm, cheer, and tranquillity. It asserted nothing and conveyed everything. And it is precisely this almost eerie self-possession that creates such an oddly compelling itch. What flora and fauna live in this place? What does it want us to see? Why, when I am so hyper, is this damned wine so calm?

This is by no means to cast aspersions on those wines that are deliberately and explicitly great. Far from it. But such wines *come at you.* They are not ambiguous, nor do they hint or imply; they come straight to the point. They are great. And that is, of course, a very good thing.

But to return to Dönnhoff, with few exceptions I don't think this can be said of his wines. They are difficult to study because they don't hold still; they are too busy melting. They don't thrust at you from any particular angle; rather, they invite you to enter a larger nexus that includes them but doesn't stop at them. Diel's Goldloch is the tower of a great gothic cathedral, mighty and filigree, rising to a definite point that the eye follows up into the sky. But when I think of Dönnhoff I think of the peaceful little cloisters nearby, and the deliberate birds who live in their shady air.

This has to do with texture, but not only with texture. I have no idea whether Helmut Dönnhoff would endorse any of this—I suspect he thinks I have a screw loose—but neither do I think there is any formula that can explain his wines. One can try, certainly; is it harvest selection, method of pressing, choice of yeast, temperature of fermentation, choice of aging container, cellar temperature, all of the above, none of the above—all *and* none of the above? Or shall we simply admit the mystery of how a wine with such unearthly glassy smoothness can also contain so much information?

However, it isn't information that will answer my questions or yours. It will instead pose even more inscrutable ones, because the wine is seldom what we'd call "intense"; it doesn't land with huge impact, but instead envelops you in a sort of tenderness you cannot identify, isolate, or explain.

There is something sapid and companionable about such wines. They don't talk only to your senses; they talk to your *life*. They seem almost entirely without affect. They are serene in themselves, numinous in their very lack of thrusting and pushing. They are all of the reasons we should love wine, but few of the reasons we actually do. We are busily determined to place our pleasure on a scale, locked in our solitary confinements. It's all about us.

I have never tasted a Dönnhoff wine and felt that it was out to thrill me or to "entertain" my senses. It simply expresses the pure honesty of itself. It hasn't a thing to prove. You almost can't believe it exists, because there's no GPS to get you there, no recipe you can follow to create *that* result. It isn't like arriving, it isn't like winning or prevailing or mastering; it is in some strange way like breathing, or daydreaming. At the end of H. G. Wells's lovely novel *The History of Mr. Polly*, the hero, who has spent his life urging and asserting, has finally learned to admit contentment into his life. We find him "not so much thinking as lost in a smooth still quiet of the mind." I think that when we look back on our lives we will know those were the times we were happiest.

Here's another way to view it. The idea of "forest" is different from the notion of "a lot of trees." The notion of "a lot of individual tones and pitches arranged in organized and pleasing ways" is existentially different from the idea of "music." "Landscape" is different from the hills and rivers it might contain. There are wines that live in the Whole, which is not only greater but also *other* than the sum of its parts. Yet it often seems that wine trains us to examine and live inside the parts. And when certain wines come along shining with their Whole-ness, we've never been taught how to respond. That's because this "Whole-ness" is very real and almost impossible to explain.

One year at Dönnhoff we had something to negotiate, and

I made a second visit in order to do so. A colleague was with me, and Helmut brought the wines out for us to taste. I passed through them unthinkingly, busy with our conversation, rather like the commuters who didn't hear Joshua Bell in the subway station that morning. Yet luckily for me, a wine found a seam and soaked through it, and suddenly I was invaded by silence. It was a tiny, lovely moment, nothing dramatic at all. But it asked a question I like to remember: *And what of this?*

My wife likes to remember her dreams, and I find this quite endearing but don't at all share it. It seems ordinary enough that our subconscious hums and buzzes all the time and we see it only when our waking consciousness is out of the way, just as we see stars only in a dark sky. But the stars are always there even when we don't see them, just as the dreams are always there even when we don't dream them. And there are wines that speak to the dreams and the stars and the beauty that is always there.

I love the phrase *vini di meditazione*. There are take-a-brisk-walk wines and there are sit-still-and-be-quiet wines. When you're out on a hike and you've walked a while and you stop to take a drink of water, the world rearranges itself. Suddenly you see leaves fluttering and grasses dancing and critters crittering, all the things you don't notice when you're making tracks. It's funny how glad you can be, as William Stafford wrote, when all you have is the world.

The truth is that I don't know how certain wines are like this, I don't know why, and I am very sure if I did know I still wouldn't know how they get that way. What I do know, or think I know, is that while brilliance, explicitness, and assertiveness are wonderful things for wines to have, there's a point at which they *stop;* they're only an amusement, even if sometimes a very fine and even noble one. The wines that go deepest seem to steal over you. You're prepared to admire them or to deconstruct them appreciatively, but these oddly haunting wines don't care what you think or feel. Something materializes out of the ether, something you knew but forgot was there.

My friend the wine writer David Schildknecht is fond of quoting F. H. Bradley's saying that metaphysics is the finding of bad reasons for what we believe on instinct. I like the quote too, especially when we're trying to clarify the inexplicable. My point here is not to explain these slippery ambiguities, but rather to pause before them and ask why they visit us and what they want.

There is a kind of beauty that is unconcerned with whatever pleasure it gives us. If and when we are aware of this beauty, it can lead to a rare kind of gratefulness, a compassion that isn't sentimental. It says that the world finds you when you are prepared to admit it, but will assault you if you are not. It says that we are not merely life-support systems attached to a taste motor. We are humans who can bring our entire selves to a glass of wine. In the quiet of these calm, exquisite wines we hear a kind of divinity. And we see that the world is charged with it—it is, we are, the current that passes between us is. And it is *always* there.

And loveliest of all, you don't have to attain this by dint of some tremendous effort or "spiritual practice"; you don't have to meditate or hold séances or even do yoga. You just have to be willing to relax and step out of your damned life for a few minutes. Nor will this make you a beatific and benign person. It's not about "self-improvement." I'm as cranky as the next guy. All it will do is stop you from wasting too much of your little brief life.

There is a saying that the last notes of a piece of music are the silence that follows the final note. Robert Frost said that if a book of poems has twenty-four poems in it, the book itself is the twenty-fifth. There are wines that let us hear the beat of time between the tick and the tock. It hardly matters how they got that way; it matters that the world includes them, and we respond. For we are all prisoners, listening to music.

five

PRESSING HOT BUTTONS

Is All Taste Equally Valid? A Defense of Elitism

The question of "validity" arises in matters of taste only when one struts one's democratic cred by claiming that one man's taste is as good as another's. The idea for this chapter came from a magazine article by a wine journalist who had a moment of awakening in which his idea of taste dilated to include *tout le monde* in its sentimental embrace. Anyone with intellectual aspirations knows this feeling, the groping toward the common touch, as if dropping your *g*'s and drinking beer from the can will transform you into someone socially and sexually desirable. Show me someone who insists that all taste is equally valid and I'll show you someone who doesn't know he isn't discussing taste—he's discussing himself.

How, after all, can taste even touch on validity? Taste is either fine or coarse, cultivated or heedless, even *good* or *bad* (and often good and bad within the same person), but "valid"?

Two things are valid. First, hierarchies exist throughout

nature, and when hierarchies exist, then so do elites. The lion is the "elite" among carnivores. Second, we're all expert at something, and we manage very often to contemplate expertise without screaming about snobbery or elitism. If we approve of the field in question, we respect the elite in that field. "Albert Pujols is one of the game's elite hitters." No one quakes at the word *elite* in this context; Albert's a hitting machine, and he's one of a tiny, select group at the top of his field. If instead we fundamentally disapprove of a subject, then expertise seems egregious: *I feel inferior before this subject, so I'll accuse you of being an elitist snob for caring about it at all.* "The intellectual elite in the foreign policy field suggest that negotiations are more productive than may at first be apparent." Oh, right, ivory-tower snobs who never had to change a tire; who cares what *they* think?

One evening at a ball game, I had the good fortune to sit next to one of the advance scouts who attend every game, gathering intel on the players for the next team they'll face. It was a slow night, and I asked if he could think out loud for me, tell me what he saw. Turns out he watched a whole different ball game from the one I did. I sat in admiration of his trained eye. I'd thought the game was exciting, and said so. "It was actually a poorly played and managed game," he responded. "Not one of baseball's finer examples." When I pressed him to elaborate, he opened a new world for me. I didn't feel inferior or rebuked; I felt educated. And I realized again the value of training and discernment.

Did I see all subsequent baseball games through these newly expanded eyes? In fact, no. Sometimes I *liked* watching the game like a simple fan. But now I'd been given a choice, to see the game analytically or as simple entertainment.

Similarly, when I take my car to a mechanic, he hears different things in the engine's hum than I do. A piano tuner hears minute tonal variances to which I am effectively deaf. A massage therapist discerns muscle tensions of which I'm not consciously aware. All of these are examples of expertise we take for granted. And yet if someone asserts expertise in wine, we are promptly suspicious; we sniff for snobbery, we get defensive. Why?

As I've discussed, wine writers often feel a degree of responsibility to "demystify" wine in order to make it accessible to everyman. That way, they reason, more people will drink it and the world will be improved. If some people like trashy wine, be gentle with them; they may grow into appreciation for the kinds of wines *we* like. Maybe, maybe not. I rather think that innate taste will show itself apart from experience. Would we argue that today's Burger King diner is tomorrow's Thomas Keller aficionado? "Let's applaud them for just being in a restaurant at all!" It seems improbable, this logic.

Other wine writers want to reassure you that there are no "rules" and that you should always just drink what you like: reasonable advice on the face of it. If you like drinking young Barolo with a dozen raw oysters, I won't stop you (though I'll shudder to think what's going on inside your mouth). If you like a cognac with a fistful of sardines steeped in it for twenty minutes, go on and drink it that way. No one wants to keep you from the consequences of your perverse taste. No one denies your right to it.

Some of us, however, like to call things by their proper names. Not from snobbism, sadism, or any other ism, but because it helps to order the world of experience. It fends off the chaos. And whatever expertise we may have attained in the things we love, there are plenty of other things to humble us. We're all on both sides of this divide all the time. I have a fascination with fragrance and am a fledgling amateur of perfumes and colognes. I thought I had good taste, because it was mine! Then I read some of Chandler Burr's writing about perfumes and colognes and was nonplussed to learn that he found many of my favorites quite despicable, and a few that he lauded to the skies were scents I found repugnant. It's self-evident that we perceive things through subjective membranes, and even if tannic red wine and shrimp conspire to produce a strong metallic flavor in the mouth, I'm sure someone somewhere *likes* that flavor and resents being hectored about its undesirability.

If you like Twinkies, eat them. Don't apologize. Have all the fun a Twinkie delivers. But don't claim it's just as good as a home-baked brownie from natural fresh ingredients, or that anyone who believes otherwise is a food snob. *It's only sugar and chemicals, but I like it.* I'm sort of a cultured guy, and yet I can't abide opera, whereas I have a perverse tolerance for professional wrestling. Again, we're all admixtures of high and low tastes, and this is fine, as long as we don't confuse them.

I had a conversation on an airplane recently with a cellist in her twenties. We talked about music, naturally, and it became clear to me that her tastes were wider than my own. (I'm an ossified old geez in his mid-fifties.) I remarked upon her ecumenical listening habits. "Well," she said, "don't you think one should search for the virtues in everything?" Much as I yearned to say yes, to do so would have been false. Instead I said: "No, I think *you* should seek the good in everything; that's where you are in your life. But what I need to do is identify that which annoys or wounds me, and avoid it."

Wine writer Stuart Pigott once wrote, "We should . . . start making wines with balance, elegance and originality sound so astonishing that our readers feel they've just got to try them," and this of course is true. Critics must stand for something; otherwise we are merely pusillanimous. The first task is to find the good and praise it. But anytime we take a stand *for* something, we imply the thing's shadow; that is to say, the thing we love suggests—it can't be helped—the thing we don't. And we must not shrink from naming both things, especially not for fear of wounding the delicate sensibilities of the philistines (who, by the way, are robustly insensitive and also have no scruples about insulting *us* with labels such as "snob" or "elitist"). God knows we'd prefer to be everyone's best friend, and we feel humane and generous telling those with unformed (or simply atrocious) taste that their taste is as good as anyone else's. But it's a lie we tell so that *we* can feel noble, and furthermore it is unfair to the recipient, who, if he's being patronized, is entitled at least to know it.

But this does not confer any sort of carte blanche to offer gratuitous insults. Good-taste bullies may have better taste than bad-taste bullies, but they're still abhorrent. Making clear distinctions in matters of taste does not grant license to be arrogant or inhumane.

Pigott went on to claim that any wine anyone likes is ipso facto "good" wine, and this is just the slippery slope we can't help sliding down when we try to be "democratic." It is manifestly impossible to support a definition of *good* as "wine that someone, regardless of who it is, finds to taste good." This is irresponsible and it ducks the question. Once at a presentation I was terribly busy and opened bottles without a chance to screen them. A punter remarked that a particular wine was "fantastic;

I never had anything that tasted like this, wow, how was this made?" His enthusiasm infected me, and I poured myself a taste. Corked! What should I have done, based on Pigott's definition of *good?* The gentleman liked a wine that was patently flawed. He has every right to like it; no one disputes this. But I felt honor-bound to (discreetly and tactfully!) correct him.

Thus I can't endorse a definition of *good* that is as inclusive and democratic as Pigott and others desire. I do not believe nature has any use for our democracies. Some things *are* better than others, and one of our functions is to guide our readers toward appreciation of these distinctions as gracefully as we're able.

If we take these democratic principles and apply them to any other thing about which aesthetic or cultural criticism is warranted, do they stand up? Shall we endorse a statement such as "All art is good art as long as someone likes it"? Does this sentiment apply equally to architecture, poetry, cuisine? Or is wine somehow "special" because too few people drink it? And should we pander to every sort of unformed or misguided taste because we're trying to get more people to drink wine?

Let me be clear: no one has to like wine the way I like it, or the way any "expert" likes it. If wine is a casual beverage for you, then the discussion ends. Wine is complicated and therefore intimidating, but I'll make you a deal: you promise not to lash out at me for what I know because you feel intimidated, and I'll promise not to guilt-trip you into acquiring expertise in a subject you don't care that much about.

Writers are well advised to write humanely, because it is good to be humane. Any professional who uses words does well to shade them so as not to deliver gratuitous insults to people with dubious or uneducated taste. But that doesn't mean he abrogates responsibility to exercise the entire range of his judgmental faculties—which by the way are *why he was hired*—in search of some romance about inclusion or democracy.

There are no "invalid" moments of pleasure in wine. But there are higher and lower pleasures. Once you have graduated from the low you can always return. It's fun to return! You *should* return, frequently, because it's good to stay in touch with your inner redneck, or you risk your taste becoming precious. But if you're in the process of honing your wine taste, and you want to continue, no one helps you who fails to delineate the distinctions among inadequate, ordinary, good, fine, and great—or between mass-produced "industrial" wines and small-scale "agricultural" wines.

Maybe there *is* a thin line between this and Pigott's concern that we will insist on our notion of high quality as an imperative. But the way through asks us to remember to be kind (or at least, not unkind) and to hone our craft with words. I feel it is indeed unkind to flatten all taste to a specious equality, made even more pernicious by encouraging the philistines to set the level.

I have a powerful aversion to prefab wines and to wines that gush and scream; they annoy me, I tell you why, and you make up your own mind. My imperative isn't everyone's, but I strive to send clear signals, to advocate what I think is worthy and to identify and explain what I think is unworthy. If my tone is (in Pigott's terms) "superior, even dictatorial," then the fault lies with me. I have failed to communicate my point.

But the point remains. Taste moves along a continuum of discernment and refinement. Each of us moves as he can, and as he wishes. It is helpful to delineate all the places along the way, and it's helpful to recall that when we cherish the best—the "elite"—in a given field it is a gesture not of snobbery, but of love.

"What's All the Fuss? Wine Is Only Fermented Grape Juice"

Aaahhh . . . right. That's all it is. And Mount Everest is just a really big pile of rock. And *Crime and Punishment* is just a long story about a student who whomps some old lady upside the head with an ax. You know, I agree with you; life is just too damn good. I'll be right there to help you suck all the blood out of every possible transcendent moment just so we can make our lives even more diminished and paltry. But let's work fast, 'cuz I've got tickets to the ball game.

But look: the batter swings and the ball rises in a soaring arc (its whiteness looks so lovely against the black sky . . . but no, it's just a hard-hit ball, keep calm, damn it) and jeez, all forty-something thousand people sitting here are suddenly on their feet watching the little ball fly, and when it lands in the seats in deep left field they all start cheering and high-fiving their neighbors and, I mean, come *on*: what possible joy can derive from this? The twenty-five overpaid athletes who happen to play in my town are now likelier to defeat the twenty-five overpaid athletes who play in *your* town, and for this I am ecstatic?

We care because we want to. We care because human beings are *made* to care. Caring feeds a hunger. Caring affirms our lives. It doesn't matter what we care about, whether bridge or crossword puzzles or lacrosse or twelve-tone music or sitcoms or sustainable agriculture or gardening or wine. Wine at least rewards our caring by giving so much back: family, culture, hospitality, beauty. And wine is entirely tolerant. You don't have to care if you don't feel it naturally. Care a little or care a lot, your wine will meet you wherever you are. But don't let anyone—let me emphasize this: *anyone*—tell you not to care, or that caring makes you some kind of geek. Everyone's a geek about something, so don't be meek, embrace the geek.

Pointless Scores

It won't hurt to repeat this: point systems, any of them, may or may not be useful in strict consumerist terms. They are probably useful or they wouldn't have metastasized as they have, though the system of thought they enforce is a feedback loop in which the reader is infantilized and thus comes to depend on the score. But we'll leave that aside for the moment. I agree for argument's sake that scoring systems are attractive to the wine consumer who wants a shorthand buyer's guide. But no scoring system can possibly work in holistic terms, because there's an inherent problem with the notion of "perfection" and because wine is not only judged, it is also *used*, and enjoyed, in many and varied ways.

To use one example, are riper wines inherently better than less-ripe wines *because* of their additional concentration? What possible answer can there be except *It depends?* Maybe the answer is yes if one is obliged to score on an absolute scale, but certainly not if one permits relativity and equivalence to enter the equation; for instance, a zippy, light Sancerre can be a "perfect" wine with oysters for which the higher-scoring wine is too concentrated.

The question of perfection is more difficult because when we feel intense pleasure, it is so awfully tempting to think, *This is as good as it gets.* But the quest for perfection is useless; it takes us down myriad blind alleys, it sticks us in a maze and then lies to us about where we are. There's little question that a *very* thin line can exist between the perfect and the bland when it comes to wine. It's not that the flaw needs to be forgiven; it's the opposite. We like the flaw (or so-called flaw) because it makes the thing interesting, animate, approachable. I mean, my Christmas tree is a little droopy on one side, and it's definitely not as picturesque as a fake tree would be, but it smells so good, and it's alive. If perfection is attainable, then it can't be miraculous, only improbable. The assumption of imperfection is the precondition for the miracle.

But buyer's guides aren't concerned with miracles; they just want to throw a lifeline to busy consumers who don't know what to buy or whether they can trust their local retailer to tell them. Fair enough. But must the scales be (or appear to be) so exact? Back when Pierre Rovani worked with Robert Parker, I asked him why it wouldn't suffice to simply have groups—fair/good/very good/excellent/superb—and rank the wines in order of preference within those groups. "Good question," answered Pierre, "so what you're proposing is a five-point scale." Touché! Hoist on my own Bâtard. My mistake was to debate the issue on the terms of the point defenders, whose logic is self-enforcing and circular. Critics have a responsibility to take a definite stand, and scoring forces them to do so. They can't hide behind vague or nebulous language. The wine is an 88, and that's all there is to it. Please read my prose too, they say, because that's where I get to use all my flavor associations and groovy locutions, but the score's the mojo.

The role of the critic in this Weltanschauung is to handicap the entrants and tell you who won the race and by how many lengths. It's all very clear, and its intentions are benign. And its logic isn't false, only incomplete.

First, any point system misleads in direct proportion to its affect of precision. The more exact, the more misleading. We all know that wine is a moving target. Even industrial wine, made to be predictable, is a moving target. Why? Because *we* are a moving target. We feel differently on different days, at different times of day. Our bodies are changeable, our palates are changeable. The overly tart salad dressing we ate at lunch will affect every wine we taste all afternoon. It doesn't matter how responsible we try to be; the moment we assign an absolute value to a wine, we have misled. And the more specific we purport to be, the more we mislead.

Yes, experienced professional tasters will allow for the variables I cited (and others I didn't cite), but even if they wanted to give themselves a little wiggle room, their hands are tied if they're selling *omniscience*. Every time someone asks Robert Parker if he has ever made a mistake or changed or regretted a score, I have to laugh. Ask the oracle all you like whether his advice or predictions are ever false, but he won't remain the oracle if he answers, "Oh, well . . . yes, my advice has sometimes proved unwise." Oh, really? Then why should I listen to it? To remain credible you have to affect (or feign) omniscience, and wine does not welcome omniscience. So we have some cognitive dissonance.

Let's also remember we're setting an example for readers, whom we are training to consider wine in terms of how many points to "give" it, and this is mischievous at best. Even if I yield the point that scores are a necessary evil—which, by the way,

I don't—how many innocent consumers of wine journals are savvy enough to know that the writer may have to use points but the *reader* doesn't? Sadly, the metamessage of point obsession is that "scoring" wines is the sine qua non of wine appreciation.

Oh, lighten up, I hear you say. What's the harm? The harm is subtle because its symptoms appear mild, but the long-term effects are pernicious.

Here's a quote I like, from John Berger's essay "The White Bird": "The aesthetic moment offers hope that we are less alone, we are more deeply inserted into existence than the course of a single life would lead us to believe." Wine is just such an aesthetic moment. It doesn't have to be great wine, it only has to be *true* wine, connected not to the factory but to the family, not to the lab but to the earth. We're invited to respond with our souls, for wines like these will open doors by which we enter a larger world than we normally inhabit. All we need is to be available for the experience.

But we will squander this opportunity if, in that very moment, we are scrolling through our egos to see how many points we're going to "award" the wine. Has no one noticed how suspiciously pompous even the language is? "We *awarded* Château Bluebols *xx* points on our 100-point scale." How nice for you. How many points did the wine give *you*, Ace? Is the whole thing really about *you?* Does the cosmos really care at all how many points you bestowed upon some mere wine? That wine was a *gift* to you, and all you can do is "evaluate" it as if it were a DVD player or a Dustbuster.

Among the various online wine bulletin boards this is a hot topic, as you might suppose. I remember one gentleman writing (and I'm paraphrasing now) that he grew *into* using the 100-

point scale when he felt his palate was mature enough. This poor lamb is running blindly toward the cliffs.

Ah, but maybe he's right. After all, I've been using the 100-point scale to assess literature ever since I turned fifty. I'd finally read enough to know exactly how good stuff was. I give Molly Bloom's soliloquy at least a 94. That ranks it among the great literary scenes of all time, along with Stavrogin's confession (95), Levin's day with the threshers (97), Gerald's walk to his death in the mountains (94+), and the death of Ben Gant (99). I didn't used to give scores to great scenes in literature. But eventually I came to realize that all pleasure was in effect a commodity, and I *owed* it to myself to quantify the little suckers. So now, when I read novels, I'm constantly thinking, *How many points is this scene worth?* I judge on imagery, diction, overall rhetoric, whether it advances the plotline and/or develops the characters, and finally on how close it brings me to tears. Eyes barely moist gets 90. Eyes barely moist plus a catch in the throat gets 91–92. Eyes full of tears but no drippage gets 93–94. Between one and three tears slipping down my face earns a 95–96, and full-bore blubbering earns the highest scores. Since I started doing this I have just gotten so much more from all these great books!

Why stop at books? Let's declare all of our pleasures subject to a precise analysis of their *extent* on an absolute scale. Then we can see what 100-point *joy* is about. "I can't possibly be happier than this"—are you *sure?*

Perhaps we're at cross-purposes. I'd rather that wine writers tried to deepen people's love of wine, but they do what they can and what they've trained their readers to expect. Robert Parker may be a convenient target for my frustration, but the truth is more complicated because he has done the wine world enormous good over his storied career, more good than whatever harm he may have caused. But I also believe, as St. Peter opens the gates to admit Mr. Parker, he'll peer through Bob's valise, pull out the folder marked "The 100-Point Scale," and say, "I'll just hold on to this. You won't be needing it here."

"Globalization" in Wine: Menace or Straw Man?

Fifty years from now it may seem quaint that a single critic wielded so much power, let alone that he became the crux of a contention that wines around the world, fashioned to appeal to his taste, were all beginning to taste the same. The shorthand for this complicated question is "globalization." A lot of people fear it's a threat to the very existence of fine wine. Other people dismiss it as a slogan for a polemic. Reason abides on both sides of this issue—to a point.

If you still doubt that civil discourse is in mortal peril, just take a peek at how this discussion is carried on, especially on the Internet. I shall try, in my uniquely unctuous fashion, to state the case for both sides and see if there's any common ground.

In my wilder fantasies I allow myself to believe this book might be read many years from now, and in the unlikely event that I am right, I wonder how readers in the future will see this issue ramify, if it does at all. Will wines have become stultifyingly homogeneous? Will the very name Robert Parker be anything beyond a historical blip? For it is Mr. Parker who, fairly or unfairly, has become the lightning rod for this tussle, and because I do admire (and like) him, I wish I could say he has risen to the occasion and comported himself with the civility incumbent upon a grand elder of the wine world. Alas, he hasn't. Each time he has written about this issue, whether in magazines (his own or others') or on his Web board, his many reasonable points are frequently diminished by a tone of defensiveness, invective, and name-calling. Persons taking views contrary to his are accused of membership in the "pleasure police" (since evidently they, unlike Parker, have a taste for wines that don't give pleasure?), peering over our collective shoulders to ensure we're all drinking lots of tight-lipped Calvinist wines. He has also trotted out that hoariest of labels, "pseudo-intellectual," to characterize his opponents. Curious. Granting the point that pseudo-intellectuals actually do exist, so do bona fide intellectuals, and I wonder how Mr. Parker tells them apart.

Wherever there is power there's also resentment of power, and a lot of power has accrued to Robert Parker. Most of the criticisms lobbed his way are unwarranted, and many of them are the incoherent irritations of people without a fraction of Parker's experience and essential seriousness. Yet some of the challenges have merit.

A few years ago, a very fine book was published, Lawrence Osborne's *The Accidental Connoisseur*, in which, under the guise of a search for "taste," the author raised the issue of whether wines the world over were endangered by a kind of uniformity of type. He did it obliquely and with exquisite slyness, and raised only the faintest of ripples. Who, after all, reads books?

Shortly thereafter a friend of his (and mine) named Jonathan Nossiter made a film called *Mondovino* that tackled the same question, this time with direct and polemical passion. Now the fur was flying. People see movies. Nossiter was accorded all the horror and loathing invited by anyone who challenges the basic orthodoxy of his time. Much of the criticism was petulant and insulting, as it often is when one strikes a nerve.

But *why* would this issue strike a nerve? My usual theory is that we overreact when we feel something we value is threatened. But the style of wine that makes Osborne, Nossiter, and myself uneasy is so prevalent that no reasonable person could claim it's under any kind of siege. No, there's some shadow here. There is reason on both sides of this dialectic, but the argumentative tone from one side tends toward hectoring and bullying, and their argument is strong enough that such tactics are unwarranted. Unless some people simply are bullies and never learned how to disagree respectfully. Interesting, then, their taste for bellicose wines. . . .

I'll try to summarize each camp's position. My biases are clear, but I have empathy for the other side, and I think they deserve better than the voice they themselves have often used. First, to define the term: *globalization* denotes a phenomenon in which wines from around the world are striving toward a similar formula, in order to appeal to Mr. Parker's taste. (This is perhaps a misuse of the broader term *globalization*—though there are concerns over multinationals in the wine world—but it has been appropriated as a shorthand term for the basic debate.) The formula, as I understand it, favors a lot of ripeness (and the high alcohol it brings) and overtly expressive flavor, *gushing* flavor in many cases, along with a certain sheen, a lashing of oak, a sense of "sweetness" based not on residual sugar but on what's called phenolic or "physiological" ripeness, achieved when the grape's skins and stems are ripe. These wines tend to be straightforward, symmetrical, and generous—and pleasurable in basic sensual terms. *Hedonistic* is an adjective much beloved among proponents of this wine style. Who doesn't like hedonism?

Globalization's critics are suspicious that wine is becoming too uniform, and they worry about the rote application of formulas or recipes to bring about the prevailing styles. They wonder whether the quirky or idiosyncratic wines they like are in danger of being crowded out by the new buxom starlets from hither and yon. For the sake of brevity, I'll call these folks "romantics."

Proponents of globalization—let's call them "pragmatists"— argue that wine in the aggregate has never been better, and that good wines are now hailing from a greater variety of places than ever before. They do not perceive a problem, and think a bunch of fussbudgets are trying to rain on their picnic.

I don't believe it's reasonable to deny their argument. There are certainly many more competent and tasty wines (and concomitantly fewer rustic, dirty, or yucky wines) than there were twenty years ago. The romantics' argument would be stronger if it conceded this point. The floor has been raised, and wine overall is the best it has ever been.

But even if the floor *has* been raised, has the ceiling been lowered? The romantics fear it has. They also fear that the pragmatists are too concerned with results and less concerned with how the game is played, as long as they are entertained. During the height of this argument the steroids scandal hit baseball, threatening the integrity of the sport. But too little attention is paid to the role we ourselves play in bringing such things about. We'd rather wish it all away. Honestly, a lot of us *enjoy* the spectacle of Herculean demigods bulked up on chemicals hitting baseballs five hundred feet. This becomes our ideal, and players who embody the ideal command the highest salaries and put the most butts in the seats. They're also the envy of other, less "enhanced" players, some of whom seek to climb aboard the gravy train.

The metaphor is temptingly apt. There is no doubt that the prevailing recipe for modern wines with commercial aspirations is easy to apply and effective at churning out ripe, sweet wines with softly embedded tannin, large-scale and concentrated, regardless of where they came from or what grapes made them. I believe the pragmatists care less about how such wines get that way than they do about being titillated and thrilled by juiced-up slugger wines hitting flavor out of the park.

Should we conduct this discussion in grayer shades? Quite possibly. Parker has often expressed his admiration for moderate, elegant, temperate wines. He typically scores them in the high eighties, and he has told me he wishes more people prized and drank such wines. Yet he must be aware that the commodity called a "Parker score" effectively damns such wines with faint praise. And although Parker himself might admire them well enough, he reserves his love and his most emotional prose for their bigger, more "hedonistic" cousins.

Thus a particular idiom becomes the prevailing idiom, because everyone wants the scores and the financial juju they engender. And superficially, this flavor idiom is persuasive, though it is at best singular and at worst predatory of other flavor idioms. The romantics struggle against the monofaceted and bland. They (we) are innately wary of uniformity, as it is contrary to nature. We're also alert to an insidious effect uniformity can create. We risk becoming passive, infantilized, dulled;

when all things are a single way, there's less reason to pay attention, as they can't surprise us anymore.

The pragmatists will claim I'm overstating the case; none of them argues that all wines should taste the same. (Few of them see that many wines *are* starting to taste distressingly similar.) Fair enough. Yet they often accuse romantics of wishing to return us to some imagined Eden of dirty, weird, and rustic wines—which, they sneer, we excuse by citing terroir. It's the classic war of straw men. Is there a sane way through?

I ask the pragmatists to consider this question: How, in a world of wines made by an indisputably prevailing set of practices in pursuit of a predictable result, will there still be room for the quirky, the angular, the evocative—the heirloom varieties of the wine world? Or are we content to let such wines disappear? Is this the wine world—is it the *world*—we wish to live in? If not, how do we prevent it?

I place no value judgments on "modern" methods per se, many of which are benign. But some amount to outright falsification. Yet this isn't the time to inveigh against even those— some people think it's fine for ballplayers to use steroids. I'm asking the pragmatists to consider the consequences inherent in their belief system. It's certainly true that good wine's coming from many regions that were unknown and unavailable twenty years ago. Yet to my palate this signifies very little, for many of these wines join an international glom of hot-climate wines whose effect calls to mind the old British phrase "much of a muchness." So there's yet another source for the same kind of wines we already have plenty of. I'm not sure why I should care.

And much of what we see from these new sources is little

more than plausibly attractive in a style we already know. It took the Old World many hundreds of years of trial and error to learn which varieties and what kind of winemaking would best capture terroir. The New World displays its customary derring-do, and presumes it can learn these lessons in the first thirty years. It can't. There are no short cuts.

In cuisine there comes a point of ennui when all you see are the same luxury ingredients in nearly interchangeable preparations. Monday it's squab stuffed with foie gras in a truffle *nage;* Tuesday it's squab stuffed with truffles in a foie gras emulsion; Wednesday it's truffle-crusted foie gras in a squab jus, and eventually it becomes a meaningless farandole of dishes constituting the "luxury dining experience," which you could have in Hong Kong or Los Angeles or Las Vegas or New York or Kuala Lumpur. It becomes a membrane separating you from the world, swaddling you in a specious bliss, seducing your senses, starving your soul. I think of this when I taste yet another big wine indistinguishable from myriad other big wines, and yes, it might well be superior to the odd little wine that grew there before—*might* be—but what does it signify? That people in lots of different places can suss the formula and apply it? I'm not sure why I should care.

Thus it doesn't really matter that good wines are coming from a greater number of places than ever, if most of those wines are cut from the same pattern. A mere grape or place-name we haven't seen before is immaterial unless the wine offers a *taste* we haven't tasted before. That's the crux of the romantics' argument.

Sometimes in our righteous passion, we romantics can also forget to be reasonable. We *must* yield the point that the floor has indeed risen for wine quality, and this is a good thing. Our struggle is to applaud this while also protecting the ceiling. And that "ceiling" isn't merely new stratospheres of hedonism (even *more* ripe fruit, even *more* intensity, always *more*), but instead it is those wines that are uniquely great, and significantly unique. There are very good Syrahs and Cabernet Francs coming from Switzerland's Valais, but these offer less to cherish than the singular and remarkable Humagne Blancs and Amignes—which don't grow anywhere else, and which taste lovely.

What other great wine is great as the best Loire Chenins are great? As the best Barolos? As the best Jurançons, the best Nahe Rieslings, the best grand cru Chablis, the best Grüner Veltliners? Ultimately it isn't greatness we must protect, it is uniqueness. Preserve the unique, and greatness takes care of itself.

Here's how it happens. To the extent that drinkers value distinctiveness in our wines, the people who make them will learn there's a market for their *particular* wines, and we'll have fostered a community of vintners who cherish what is uniquely theirs. This doesn't mean all of their wines will be great. But it is the basis, the prerequisite for greatness.

The pragmatists would do well to remember the risks inherent in their aesthetics. And we romantics need also to realize we *have* misapplied the concept of terroir to excuse feeble or flawed wines. This concept is precious, and we need to respect it and use it with care. And we romantics have sometimes been guilty of a form of Puritanism; if it tastes unpleasant, it must be virtuous.

But the pragmatists ought to acknowledge that theirs isn't the only form of pleasure. There are worlds alongside the sensual. Wine can be intellectually and even spiritually nourishing. People can desire those things, and the true hedonist isn't threatened by them.

I wonder if we cannot all unite behind the value of diversity. I'd like to think so, though sometimes I despair. From my high-rise window I often see raptors soaring on the thermals, especially in fall and winter, and I love watching them swoop in elegant arcs across the sky. But I could never imagine myself feeling, *I sure love these hawks, and all the other big birds, eagles, buzzards, falcons, and it would be great if all birds were like these because they give me so much pleasure.* What about the assertive, gaudy cardinal? The pensive heron? The silly woodpecker? The delicate little finch? I want to live in a world of thousands of *different* wines, wines whose differences are deeper than zip code, each of them revealing fragments of the unending variety and fascination of this lovely green world on which we walk.

six

OF PLACES AND GRAPES

When you look at bottles of Mosel wine from the 1960s and before, even from the best vineyards, you will hardly ever see the word *Riesling*.

Burgundy labels do not contain the words *Pinot Noir* or *Chardonnay*. Vouvray and Savennières do not proclaim *Chenin Blanc*, and neither Barolo nor Barbaresco says *Nebbiolo*. The classic Old World model was always based on the *place* from which a wine hailed. We needed to learn the name of the grape.

When wine was marketed in the New World, it was first labeled with place-names to which it wasn't entitled. Thus *Chablis* was stripped of its meaning as a particular place in northern France, and diminished to a spurious synonym for white wine, just as *Sauterne [sic]* was used to denote a sweet wine. It is still being done with *Champagne*. I dream that someday a vigneron in the Languedoc will bottle something he calls Napa Valley Cabernet Sauvignon, and when the Californians react in righteous outrage, our canny hero will mildly say, "Well, you know, here in France we understand *Napa Valley* to be a generic term for any Cabernet that grows under a hot sun"—and then the fur will fly.

Later the more ambitious and conscientious New World vintners sought to distinguish themselves from the rabble who used "borrowed" place-names, and thus was born the era of varietal labeling. And consumers who began their wine education with New World items got the message that Grape Is All. Alas, in doing so they missed something crucial about wine. Burgundy is a reality apart from the grapes that happen to grow there. You'll know when you visit. It's *Burgundy*, not merely "Pinot Noir from eastern France." To focus on the grape detached from the context of place is to lose the forest for the trees.

Wine historians more erudite than I have detailed the often centuries-long, painstaking trial and error by which it was eventually understood that a particular grape seemed to make the best wines in a given spot. But we need to remember what guided the search. It wasn't only the desire for the "best" possible wine; it was also the desire to hear the voice of the land in the form of flavor. You might protest that this is just poetry, but when the land was worked by hand, the worker was closer to it, more aware of its life and of his own role in keeping it vital and healthy. Arriving at the best choice of grape is like tuning the dial on an old-fashioned radio; you tweak and shift in tiny increments, and suddenly there's a clear signal. When a grape feels at home, its voice is clear as it narrates the text the land has written.

Once the choice of grape is established and codified, one starts to look at the different ways it expresses itself in various plots of land within a region. This expression involves more than ripening alone, because the grape would not have been chosen at all if it wouldn't ripen. Vintners couldn't survive. There has to be an accord among grape, land, and person whereby all three of them know that things are in their proper places. (I realize such statements raise the hackles of some of the linear technocrats populating much of the New World, but I am at the very least *intrigued* by Michael Pollan's audacious notion in *The Botany of Desire* that we didn't choose the plants we cultivate, the plants chose us. I wouldn't insist that this is true—or True—but I'm willing to believe in a symbiosis between cultivar and cultivated whereby it's hard to recall who asked whom to the party.)

We always return to the place—because the place isn't the same as other places, and sometimes a place is different from any other place. If you are growing the same grape throughout a region, place becomes the crucial variable. Yes, I know about clonal variations in grape varieties—there are lots of small rogue variables, and more in some regions than in others. But taking, say, the Nahe region of Germany, you have basically two clones of Riesling at play, which no one could tell apart by flavor alone. But beneath the vines is a Valhalla for the amateur of locale, a geological miasma, with soil changing every few meters. Spend a day tasting Nahe Rieslings, and then try to defend the notion that grape is supremely important. Place seems to matter just as much.

All Nahe Rieslings taste like Riesling, and no one would dispute that Riesling is the best variety for the region's prevailing conditions. But the taste of Riesling per se is of little import here; it is the astonishing variation in flavors arising from one vineyard and its neighbor that fascinate us. One site may be flowery and its neighbor fruitier, and *their* neighbor more minerally, or there may be variations among fruits, flowers, and minerals, and these variations can occur in sites just a few meters apart. It seems miraculous. But it's also fun, because we humans enjoy contrasting, comparing, and cataloguing when the theme is so replete with telling distinctions. And one of the things we discover is how easily we recognize the consequences of extraordinary land. A great vineyard's wines are not merely riper; they are in every way more expressive, more complex, more beautiful. They may not be riper at all. But there is something singular about them, a libretto to accompany the varietal music.

I sometimes call this the grand cru effect, something profound that isn't derived from fruit, and where such fruit as may be present is absorbed into a deeper whole. Grand cru lands are the earth's erogenous zones, some confluence of nerve endings that tingle at the touch of sunlight. It's why the old ones didn't include the grape name on the label—the place mattered more.

If I'm asked to choose among grape varieties, or to identify the ones I think are ordinary, good, or great, I don't stop at the tastes of the wines. There are some grapes whose wines taste distressingly similar wherever they're planted, and some that taste wonderful in certain places and yucky in others. I like the temperamental ones. To cite a common example, Cabernet Sauvignon; there's no question that great wines are made from this variety (though the greatest employ other varieties as blending partners), but there's also no question that they are all great *in the same way*, regardless of where they're grown. And their innate style is so seductive that they are grown all over the place, and most of the time the place is trampled underfoot by Cabernet's overwhelming "varietality." If a decent taster can't tell a Napa Cabernet from a St. Julien, then the world has something to grieve, not celebrate.

Chardonnay is the other variety most conducive to ennui—maybe we should refer to it as *Chard-ennui*. It has certainly flooded the world with oceans of stupefyingly mundane, "spoofulated" wines. (I adore that coinage, which so perfectly evokes wines that are amped up or "pimped" with extraneous flavor designed to get high scores.) Chardonnay seems to lend itself to palate pandering, and this is a shame because there's at least one place where it speaks with profound, articulate force—Chablis. But consider: Chablis is considered an "undervalued" wine, and it's because it's too expressive and idiosyncratic for a wide market to appreciate. I sometimes wonder if a talented but inexperienced taster, given Chablis for the first time, would even know it was made from Chardonnay. I also wonder whether Chardonnay is ineluctable to the identity of Chablis. Imagine if Sauvignon Blanc and Aligoté were "promoted" from the second-class land they grow in now, and were introduced to the premier or grand crus. What if Riesling were planted in Chablis? But if we assume Chablis is what it is *because of* Chardonnay, then we have to conclude that Chardonnay is at least *capable* of greatness if it's grown where it belongs. Champagne also comes to mind, and some of the most resplendently beautiful and complex wines you can taste are old Blanc de Blancs.

But what of this silly notion of Chablis planted with Riesling? It can sometimes be difficult to separate grape variety from terroir, because terroir speaks, of course, *through* the grape, and because it is quite rare to see more than one grape planted in great terroirs. Rare, but not impossible.

Consider Austria's Wachau. This region and Alsace are the only places I can call to mind where grand cru vineyards are often planted with more than one variety, in this case Grüner

Veltliner along with Riesling. Yes, there are certain sites (most often flat vineyards on alluvial soil) where Riesling doesn't belong but where Grüner Veltliner makes at least middling-good entry-level wine. But many of the top vineyards, such as Kellerberg, Steinertal, Loibenberg, and Achleiten, are planted with both, offering the drinker a rare chance to see terroir *abstracted* from grape. And what do we see?

We see that these grand crus have identities so powerful as to supersede grape flavors—not to quash them, but to put them in their proper place. It happens that I taste Steinertal and Loibenberg each year from both varieties as rendered by the angelic Leo Alzinger. And believe me, Steinertal is *always* itself, "green," wildly herbal, piercingly limey, narrated by Riesling in this glass and Veltliner in that one. Same for the smoky, tropical-flavored Loibenberg. It compels a few of those lovely unanswerable questions that make wine such fun. If Riesling didn't exist, would we taste those Veltliners and think, *This is the perfect grape for these soils; how could anything be better?* What do the two varieties have in common that lets them transmit terroir so precisely? Is it their deep root systems and late ripening? Can we know at all? Even more curiously, Riesling was rather scarce in the Wachau until the advent of drip irrigation; the sere terraces were formerly planted with Neuburger. But when irrigation enabled Riesling to grow, grow it did, and the land found its noblest voice of all.

M y favorite grapes are those so woven into where they grow that grape and place are no longer extricable, like when you pull one thread and the whole sweater unravels. But when pressed to consider grape alone, there's no question in my mind at all which is the greatest grape, of either color: Riesling.

If there's any problem with Riesling, it's that it will spoil you for anything else. Hans Altmann of the Jamek estate in the Wachau once said, "There are times when I think that any sip of wine that isn't Riesling is wasted." Riesling is so digitally precise, so finely articulate, so pixilated and pointillist in detail that other wines seem almost mute by comparison.

And if you grow Riesling where it belongs, its wines come out of the ground already perfect. They are inimical to the diddlings of hotshot "winemakers" eager to strut their cellar chops. Riesling resists the face-lift depilation tummy-tuck breast implant school of vinification. Riesling does more than just imply terroir: it subsumes its own identity as fruit into the greater meaning of soil, land, and place. Riesling knows soil more intimately than any other grape, perhaps because it ripens so late in the fall and is thus on the vine longer than other varieties, and because it thrives in poor soils with deep bedrock strata into which it can sink its probing roots. Riesling is beloved of all who grow it for being so cooperative—the furthest thing from a diva. It survives all but the most brutal frost, is hearty in its resistance to disease, and yields well without sacrificing flavor—perhaps because it ripens late in the fall when everything is taut and crisp and golden. Riesling wines are the afterglow of the contented world.

Riesling will thrive in any idiom. Its dry wines can be superbly focused and expressive, its almost-dry wines can be even longer and more elegant in flavor, its going-on-sweet wines are the apotheosis of fruit and mineral flavor, and its truly sweet wines are uniquely piquant.

It is also food's best friend. If, from this day forward, you swore to drink nothing but Riesling and eat only the things that went with it, your diet would hardly change, unless it consists of rare unsauced red meat and eggplant Parmesan. You would also discover the wine you'd been seeking for any number of dishes you'd thought were too "difficult" for wine. Riesling wine may be the most complex in the world, but it's never boastful; it is a team player, there to make food taste better. Riesling isn't shy or demure, it is modest and tactful, but if you pay attention to it—which it never *insists* you do—you'll discover how deep these still waters run. Ironic, isn't it? The grape with the most to say is the very one that speaks in a moderate voice.

Riesling often provides two things wine drinkers need: acidity and low alcohol. Acidity is innate to the berry, and it's acidity that creates the greatest magic at the table. Low alcohol is a gift to the drinker who'd rather not to be semicomatose by the time the main course arrives. Riesling needs a certain ripeness, but once this is reached it needs no more, and its value is not demonstrated by ripeness per se. Nor do we sacrifice flavor as we appreciate Riesling's sheer drinkability. There is no wine on earth with more flavor than a tingly little Mosel Kabinett with its 8 percent alcohol.

Riesling's aging capacity is legendary; no other grape undergoes a similar metamorphosis over time. When you taste a great old Riesling you can barely infer the taste of the young wine. If you saw a butterfly without knowing whence it came, would you assume it derived from a caterpillar?

Riesling is also particular about where it's planted. It is at home in the Rheinland (Germany and Alsace) and in Austria, and there are stirring signs it may be at home in certain parts of Australia—time will tell. It doesn't pout when it's planted in "foreign" places; it just goes mute, giving a simple wine that can cloy if it's too ripe or too sweet. Riesling is aristocratic, yet it's also down-to-earth because it knows it is translating a text that was written in the ground. Its fundamental humility is reflected in the people who grow it, love it, and delight in it.

Similar claims are often made for Pinot Noir, and people who love Riesling almost always love Pinot Noir too. As do I. But the argument for Pinot Noir is clouded by the complexity of its winemaking parameters. Riesling on the other hand is simple. It begs for (and receives) a less-is-more approach in the cellar because all of its flavor is already there. You can clean the juice in different ways, though the best growers just let gravity do it instead of agitating with centrifuges, filters, or separators. You can crush and press it if you want a chewier, more tactile wine, or you can press the whole clusters if you want a gossamer, crystalline wine. You can ferment *au naturel* with ambient yeasts or else use cultured yeasts, and only the very best tasters could tell the two apart. You can make it in steel if you want to preserve the utmost primary fruit and mineral, or you can make it in *neutral* wood if you want more vinous, tertiary flavors. But these are all issues not of text, but of font.

The question of minerality is inherent to Riesling, because the variety is, in its essence, more mineral than fruit. The Riesling genre is one of a mineral-tasting wine into which are woven various strands of fruit, depending on site and vintage. But there's a lot of (sometimes willful) distortion of the M-word. It's a lightning rod for an often contentious debate that's usually conducted dishonestly.

We don't know whether the flavor we call mineral results from an actual trace of dissolved literal mineral in the wine. I personally think it doesn't. More accurately, I'm agnostic on the question, because it hasn't (yet?) been demonstrated to be true. But *something* is creating that definite, tangible flavor, and we don't know what or how. Tasters of varying types and temperaments use all kinds of phrases to describe it—"crushed rocks," "wet stones," among others. I once heard a beginner describe the taste of Champagne as like "licking the shell of an oyster," which is almost literally true: chalk is nothing more than an agglomeration of the shells and skeletons of sea creatures, and Champagne grows on chalk.

I think minerality is perhaps the noblest of flavors *because* it is metaphorical, and metaphors work on the imagination. Fruitiness, on the other hand, is a simple matter of identification—it tastes like this apple or that pear, this peach or that melon—and once you've identified it, you don't think anymore. Minerality in contrast is suggestive, even mysterious. We don't know what it is or how it got there. We grow alert to the loveliness of the unknowable.

I don't drink Riesling all the time, though I'd hardly mind doing so. Still, there are occasions when something more pagan is called for, and that's when I summon my guiltiest of wine pleasures: Scheurebe.

Scheurebe *(shoy-ray-beh)*, often shortened to "Scheu," is Riesling just after it read the Kama Sutra. Put another way, Scheu is what Riesling would be if Riesling were a transvestite. If Riesling expresses all that is Noble and Good, Scheu offers all that is Dirty and Fun. It is Riesling's evil, horny twin.

The variety arose from a crossing done in 1916 by a botanist,

Georg Scheu. It is certainly emphatic next to Riesling, but it takes what is essentially a Riesling *type* and ladles a wicked blast of sauce over it. Scheu's usual associations are pink grapefruit, sage, cassis, and elderflower, and when it isn't ripe enough you'll probably think of cat pee. But Scheu has magic tricks it won't explain. However blatant it may be, it can also show remarkable class and elegance, and it will work with food for which Riesling may be too delicate. Every Asian-fusion place in the world should have fifteen Scheurebes on its list. It makes an excellent dry wine (it needs to be ripe enough or it can seem bitter), a wonderful barely sweet wine, and an amazingly exciting sweet-ish wine in which its earthy-spicy-floral thing seems to twirl the palate away from the sweetness.

Tastes differ, of course, and what's sizzling and emphatic to me might be blatant and vulgar to you, but if you love Scheu you're really in a kind of thrall to it. It has little of Riesling's spiritual depths, but neither does Riesling have Scheu's erotic power. We need both for a balanced diet. Yet however writhing and sweaty our Scheu may be, it doesn't preclude a certain poise, a certain stature, a certain . . . dare one say, aristocracy? Scheu may be blatantly flirtatious, but it's far from ignoble, and I doubt there's an equivalent in the world of wine.

Scheu will keep, but it doesn't change with age as Riesling does. It's more partial to some soils than to others, but not as sensitive as Riesling. Indeed, it enjoys conditions similar to Riesling, which is probably why we don't see more Scheu; given the choice, most vintners would plant Riesling, which has a wider audience and fetches a higher price. Scheu is almost never minerally, yet planted in a grand cru it can restrain its extravagance and offer a complexity of its own. It's fun enough to be a wine geek's guilty secret, but fine enough not to insult one's intelligence. Still, it must be said that Scheu expresses *itself* more than its place, and that's why, though it can be very good, it is almost never great.

The greatest grapes are those that carry you away, and among these is the singular and searching Chenin Blanc. An extremely finicky fellow, Chenin Blanc seems to give its best only in a small fillet of France along the Loire River and its tributaries.

If Riesling is a brilliant wine, Chenin is more *luminous;* its light softer, more dispersed. If Riesling is vigorous and energetic, Chenin is more stately. It reflects the sweet light of the place it is grown, where the most classical and perfect French is spoken, and there is a corresponding perfection in the voice of fine Chenin. It has yet to make great wine anyplace else, and there isn't all that much truly great Chenin even along the Loire. But when you find one it can be soul-expanding as few other wines—few other *things*—can be.

It's usually described in terms of quince, rosewater, and lanolin, and I often find the smell of a blown-out candle. (I remember an '82 Coulée de Serrant that smelled like a whole church's worth of blown-out candles, and I half-expected a procession of monks to parade through the dining room.) Chenin is also more yielding than Riesling, but it can't be called soft. Everything about it is allusive.

As I write I find I am also thinking about Piemonte's Nebbiolo, which offers something of the same experience. If Chenin sings of the light of the Loire with its gauzy, breathy voice, Nebbiolo sings of the fogs after which it is named, and of the earth and the animals and the dark flowers scattered over it. Truffles, violets, leather, but none of it blatant, and all of it in a murmuring thrall of beauty. Great Barolo and Barbaresco, Nebbiolo's utmost expression, are perfectly inscrutable and wonderfully mysterious. To be sure, a lot of the wines are made in modern idioms specifically to be *more* visibly and tangibly flavorsome, but the old-school wines hold a séance on your palate.

Indeed, thinking of Chenin and Nebbiolo in the same breath, I find them kin, or perhaps they are the king and queen of a rare hidden kingdom of ghosts whose dreams they allow you to hear. An old Barolo or an old Vouvray or Savennières offers an invitation with no equivalent in the world of flavor; they will take you to the wellspring, to your own wellspring. I have often felt them melt away the membrane by which I'm separated from the world. This can be unsettling.

Such wines are not easy to find. We drink them just a few times in our lives. But we never forget them, or the places they lead us to. A few weeks before writing this, I dined with my wife in the Austrian Alps, in a restaurant whose chef worked with wild local herbs. We drank two stunningly brilliant dry Rieslings that buzzed and crackled like neon, and then we drank a '93 Barolo from Bruno Giacosa, a so-so vintage but fully mature. To go from the giddy, giggling clarity of those Rieslings into the warm murmuring depths of that Barolo was moving in a way I grope to describe. It was as if the Riesling prepared us somehow, it reassured us that everything was *visible*, and then that smoky twilight red wine . . . like the moment it gets too dark to read, and you get up to turn on the light and see a tiny scythe of moon low on the horizon and you open the window and smell the burning leaves, night is coming on, and there will be dinner and the sweet smells of cooking, and then at last the utter dark, and the heart beating darkly beside you.

I did something I seldom do—got just a bit plastered that evening, for which I blamed the altitude, though I knew better. But I wasn't letting a drop of that Barolo go to waste. It stirred the deepest tenderness because it possessed the deepest tenderness. Tenderness is different from affection. Tenderness has a penumbra of sadness, or so I have always felt. Tenderness says there is an irreducible difference separating us, although we might wish to dissolve it. But we can't quite, however close together we draw; it is there as a condition of being. And then we see the sadness that surrounds us, wanting to merge into one another and finding it impossible; and then there comes a compassion, it is this way for all of us sad hopeful beings; and *then* the membrane melts away, even without touching it melts away.

I don't know how it is for other people, but I myself know a wine is great when it makes me sad. Not a bitter, grieving sadness, but the thing the Germans call *Weltschmerz*, "the pain of the world," a fine kind of melancholy.

I pause before writing about Pinot Noir, and I don't think I have much to say about it. Some have called it the "red Riesling," which makes sense. Burgundy, which is more than merely Pinot Noir, is a heartrendingly beautiful and frustratingly irregular being. Pinot Noir is difficult in the vineyard, and persnickety overall. And what sensible wine drinker doesn't love it? Burgundy is satisfying and life-affirming; I couldn't live without it, I adore it young and I love it old and when I'm a hugely successful author I'll be able to afford it more often.

Forgive my brevity regarding Pinot Noir. It is wonderful. It is suave yet rustic, polished yet earthy, intricate yet forthright, and somehow it is both sensual and, at its best, mystic. Great Burgundy seems to claw right into your viscera, yet its call is angelic. We talk about Cabernet as we talk about sports, but we talk about Pinot Noir as we talk about religion. If I could drink all the great Burgundy I ever wanted, at a price of having to forgo Cabernet for the rest of my life, I'd miss Cabernet, but I'd do it. I would not do the reverse.

And then there's my beloved Muscat. Of all the wines I know, good dry (or just off-dry) Muscat is the most lovable. I realize that love is subjective and irreducible, and that you might not love it as I do, or maybe not at all. I won't understand you, but there it is. But even knowing my drooling crush on Muscat is just me being me, I think there's a claim to stake for this variety.

Muscat can restore us to an almost primordial innocence of the senses. I was watching a young father wheeling his little boy in a stroller. He picked a dandelion and handed it to his child, who was just transfixed, grinning and beaming at the common little flower, his entire being numinous with delight. It doesn't take a great thinker to observe that we lose this quality as we grow up, just as it doesn't require a remarkable soul to miss it. But we don't have to meekly surrender. Muscat can bring it back.

When I drink good Muscat it is always one of those almost precognitive moments of recovering an embedded and inaccessible memory of how *wonderful* a thing can taste. It's as if you entered the butterfly house and suddenly all those colorful little guys were flittering around and you were dumbstruck by how comically gorgeous nature can be.

You do have to watch out, as all Muscat isn't the same. In Alsace it can be a blend of the so-called Yellow Muscat (a.k.a. the small-berried Muscat) and an inferior variety called Muscat-Ottonel, inferior by dint of its more specious perfume and softer structure. Yellow Muscat is the very bitch to grow, which tends to imply a degree of utopian fanaticism among those who brave its challenges of late ripening and uncertain yields. You can find wines made with 100 percent Gelber Muskateller (as it is called) in Germany and Austria, and they can make you weightless with happiness.

The last among my favorite varieties is, of course, Austria's Grüner Veltliner, henceforth abbreviated GrüVe. Why "of course"? Because it is a hugely important variety both for its flavor and also for its *usefulness*.

You may recall my effusions on behalf of Austria's magnificent dry Rieslings. They are her finest wines. I rejoice in each one of them I have in my cellar. And yet I drink three bottles of GrüVe for every one Austrian Riesling. Grüner Veltliner is by far the most flexible dry white wine in the world at the table. Someday a really headstrong, visionary sommelier will have only GrüVe as a dry white selection, and where food is concerned, few would miss the absence of other options (unless the menu was fusiony-eclectic and needed whites with residual sugar). GrüVe shines in so many idioms, from light wines you

gulp like springwater to medium-weight wines that just insinuate themselves to your food to big, resonant wines that offer a
profundity to partner your "important" dishes.

But can't the same be said about a dry Riesling? Said, yes, but
not defended. Dry Riesling is among the world's *more* flexible
white wines, but GrüVe overtakes it with a larger body, a more
capacious structure, and a particular set of flavors that harmo-
nize with Riesling killers. If it were Italian instead of Austrian
it would be called Valtellina Verde and the wine world would be
abuzz; finally, a truly *great* Italian white wine! Its carafe wines
would be slurped outdoors *(alfresco)* while its serious wines
would be offered for grand *(grande)* occasions. We'd also rejoice
at how well it partnered peppery, difficult salads using mizuna
or arugula *(arugula)*, not to mention going perfectly with every
veggie that's usually homicidal to wine—artichokes, asparagus,
avocado, and all the ones that stink up your house when you
cook 'em, like broccoli or cauliflower or brussels sprouts.

GrüVe seems entirely particular to Austria. It has the Vien-
nese wit and insouciance and it has the robustness and sinew
of the countryside. It is baroque in the ways the churches are.
But its wines are more corporeal than German wines, which
are more mystical. Even mature GrüVe (and the variety ages
deliberately and for a great many years), while it is thrillingly
complex, is still more *food* than ether.

GrüVe has two sets of flavor according to the soil it grows
in, though there's a degree of overlap among them. In loess (a
glacial sediment extremely rich in minerals) it goes in a "soft,"
lentilly direction. One hears talk of legume, sorrel, meadow
flowers, mimosa and oleander, rhubarb, green beans, and, if one
is fanciful, moss and heather and vetiver. On the volcanic and

metamorphic soils called primary rock, it's another story; pepper is the archetypal descriptor, along with peppery greens such as bok choy and cress. There are scents of boxwood, tobacco leaf, strawberries if it's very ripe, and a minerality so dense and compacted one thinks of ferrous ore.

GrüVe is like some hypothetical spawn from a union of Sauvignon Blanc and Viognier, with Daddy's green, flinty, herbal flavors and Mommy's flowery flavors. Yet it isn't quite literally like either. It is in fact its own ornery self, and once you encounter it, you may not be able to imagine life without it.

seven

WINE FROM OUTSIDE

Mine is not the first book by a professional wine importer, and I hope I'm not contributing to any sort of genre— "The beautiful things I've done, and the colorful people I've known. . . ." That I-focus seems to distort the experience somehow, as if it were seen in a fun-house mirror that made some of it smaller and some of it larger than it really was. But how can I be sure what it really was or, in my case, still is?

I have developed a portfolio of estates whose wines I select and advocate and sell. Every choice I've made has been for my own pleasure only, never with a market in mind. The portfolio reflects my preferences, partly from self-indulgence but also plain pragmatism, because I know I'm not a good enough salesman to push what I don't believe in. As the years passed, patterns emerged, and I began to glean an anchoring pattern from which a system of values began to arise. This book is concerned with those values. But if I consider the prosaic tasks in the work I do, selling wine and being loyal to my growers and customers, I find I feel a certain shame. It feels as if whatever I have done, it should have been more.

I am mindful of the people my work has aided. There are growers who had worked in obscurity and for whom I helped earn a worldwide reputation. There is at least one grower to whom I brought prosperity who would not otherwise have had it, a small domain that had sold nearly all its wine in bulk until I arrived, after which a great many wines were bottled for me to sell, wines that would not have existed had I not wanted them.

Time is always too short. I know a grower in Germany who is a practicing Buddhist and whose entire conversation about his land, his vines, and his wines is concerned with their "energy fields," and how his choices either block or encourage these forces. I'm agnostic about the Buddhism but enormously intrigued by the practice of mindful viticulture, and I agree the work is more authentic when the vintner feels that his land and vines are every bit as real as himself. I yearn to spend a day with this man, walking the rows of vines, naming the bugs and birds, putting our hands in the dirt, prompting him with the occasional question and hearing how it is for him. I want this, and he deserves my full attention for as much time as it takes or as much time as he's willing to give me. But when? I have sixty-nine more growers to visit, and I can't spend six months in Europe; there's wine to be sold.

I wonder about this Buddhist grower and about nearly all of his colleagues whom I represent. Do they get enough of me? Do they know I believe in them and the work they do? How do they feel when I dash away for the next appointment? What can I really say about their experience?

Individual winegrowers, of course, are as diverse as people in any profession. But over the years I've noticed a few common facets. One of them is this: however beautiful the results may be, the actual work is sweaty. I think growers everywhere enjoy a slim edge of derision regarding us aesthetes. For each of us who cherishes a bucolic fantasy of the harvest there's a winegrower whose hands are stung by bees. And so there's a fraternity of growers united by knowing things the rest of us don't know. You hear it when they talk with one another. They rarely linger over the aesthetics; they talk about *the stuff they did*, the myriad mundane details of the job.

The profession doesn't tend to attract the mystic temperament. Nor does it necessarily coddle the introvert who likes to express himself in writing. Most growers I know are more farmers than *artistes*. I've sometimes sent them questions of a searching nature, which they could ponder and answer at their leisure. It seemed reasonable, but it flirts with arrogance. I eventually learned that many growers found the questionnaire "too much like school" (which many of them hated) and, even more salient, what little free time they had was for family, amusement, recreation; answering the importer's earnest queries was a priority roughly between obtaining a root canal and scrubbing lime deposits off their shower stalls.

But I feel a city boy's guilt about my remove from the plain hard work of viticulture. If I were a grower, I'd despise me. So I seek to understand the grower's experience at the ground level—not when we're in his tasting room or making sales calls, but what his work is like when none of us is there to observe it.

Here's Mud on Your Shoes

Yesterday it was late April, and where I live we have catbirds passing through. I was walking across a numbing strip-mall parking lot when I heard the gorgeous, unearthly sound. I followed it to a tree and found the crazy bird on a low branch, indifferent to me even as I drew closer. I stood there at least ten minutes before I heard him make any single sound twice. I even called my wife and held out the phone for a few minutes. If you've never heard a catbird, you can't imagine their creativity and insouciance.

I thought of it because I've had many winegrowers tell me they like to hear the birds when they're out in the vineyards. One very rugged guy astonished me when he said he was counting the days till the nightingales would come. He seemed the kind who'd rather talk about tractors, but people will surprise you.

It is very easy to make puerile romance out of these lives. "People of the vine" is typical of the fulsome language used by dewy-eyed writers. People of the antiperspirant or the bee sting would be closer to the truth. I've spent the past quarter-century of my life doing business with winegrowers, but unlike some of my colleagues I have no ambition to make wine. I'm effete and I'll just handle the aesthetics, thanks. But I wonder whether there is a common temperament among the people who choose this work. And I wonder what rewards them.

Bear in mind, I deal in the Old World, and only with family-owned estates. Children born into winegrowing families experience a very powerful cohesion, similar to that of small-farm families. It chafes some of them. Others are indifferent, and some are attracted. Parents pay lip service to the children's right to make their own choices, and to be fair it's often more than lip service. It is by no means inevitable that the youth will follow their parents, and if they do it is a great relief. For Americans this may seem rather quaint, because part of our national mythos is the perfect right to make our own way. That current has traveled to Europe as well, and it has trickled down to the rural life. Yet they have their own mythos, having to do with the dignity of successive generations engaged in a family enterprise, and if you're a young'un who stands as the umpteenth generation in a family wine estate stretching back centuries, you need a pretty compelling reason to break the chain. Americans might feel yoked to a life they didn't choose. Europeans might discern a beauty in the passage of generations carrying the thing on. And they're both right.

Many of the growers I've worked with are now retiring and handing the estate off to a daughter or son. I'm fascinated with what informs that young person's choice. It seems improbable to me, because I don't romanticize viticulture; most of it is a pretty brusque affair. And so I ask myself, What does this life entail? Who chooses it, and why? Once chosen, what aspect brings the most satisfaction, even the most joy?

The answers are many, and some of them are obscure. I know people who seem not to have thought about it. It was "assumed" they'd carry on the winery. Yet they don't seem at all unhappy. They show no signs of yearning for the choice they didn't get to make. Perhaps they are relieved because they didn't face the crucible of self-invention. Or maybe they saw the vintner's life and liked it. In Germany, the custom is to shove fledglings out of the nest and encourage them to travel widely. Young Sebastian Strub of Nierstein's is a typical story; he spent a semester in New Zealand, went to Japan to see Strub's importer at work, did *stages* in Austria and Germany, and so when he returns to the estate to accept the reins he'll have gotten the wander-bug out of his system, and learned a few things besides. Modern young German vintners may be rural, but they aren't provincial.

Caroline Diel went another way. Her family's estate is blue-chip, and her father casts a giant shadow. Armin Diel is one of Europe's most important wine journalists, a formidable lord of the manor and of all he surveys. Caroline is smart, charismatic, very beautiful, and connected. She could have done almost anything.

She apprenticed in Burgundy and at a couple of estates in Austria, and wandered in a picaresque drift with no particular end in view. She proceeded to New Zealand, and got work with a family winery. And there she had her awakening. "It wasn't the work per se," she says, "though of course I was always interested in grape growing and winemaking. It was that I saw this young couple working at something *that belonged to them*, where they could enact their visions and build something of their own."

"What was that like?" I asked.

"I couldn't wait to get home," she said. "I mean, there it was, all waiting for me; it was mine if I wanted it." And so she returned to the tiny village of Burg Layen and began to establish herself as proprietress, no mean feat with Power Dad looming in the background. She also needed to forge her own accord with the estate's established cellarmaster and vineyard manager, whom Dad had hired. Fast-forward two years: I've arrived early for my annual visit, and Armin and I are kibitzing and fussing over all the polemical disputes of the day—the tasting can't begin until Caroline's there, you see. And in a moment there she is, clomping into the tasting room ruddy and schvitzing from the vineyards, resplendent in her heavy boots. And so we taste the new vintage between stories of how it was grown, and at some point I ask Caroline what she likes best about the work. She answers promptly, "For me, the best part is getting to know the vineyards, because you can't rush it. You really have to spend time in them to see what makes them tick."

I remembered Helmut Dönnhoff saying something similar. He'd obtained a parcel in a great site called Dellchen, and after about four years the quality of the wine took a big stride forward. I noticed it and remarked upon it, and he agreed; the new vintage had jumped ahead of all its predecessors. I asked, "Is it because the vines are older?"

"No—although they are," he replied. "I'm not sure there is a *reason*, except that I'm getting to know the vineyard better. We're more at home with each other." I can just see my concrete-minded, linear-intellect friends groaning and rolling their eyes. What's all this *mysticism?* What, indeed. Dönnhoff is about the most matter-of-fact guy I know, but he talks about this aspect of a vintner's life quite explicitly: "I hope my wines convey a *story*," he says. "Otherwise they're just things, bottles of wine, good wine certainly, but I want them to tell the story of a man in his landscape."

Is this really so nebulous? I wonder. Anyone who has ever tended a garden experiences the same thing. You get to know your garden, and it responds to you. How can it do otherwise? It might respond with vigorous growth if you're a skillful grower, or it might respond with weeds and blight if you're careless or inattentive—but respond it must. Is it such a stretch to imagine that it responds in some way to the *love* you show it? If you like being in your garden, if you observe it with interest, curiosity, appreciation, should we really insist that it *cannot* respond? Why would we rather believe that?

Of course, there are shades of temperament among growers, but the overwhelming majority of vintners I know would agree that they are happiest among the vines.

Still, with the Diels and Dönnhoffs of the world we receive something extraordinary at the end of their labors. It isn't always easy to know why or how a wine becomes extraordinary, let alone a group of wines, year after year. The notion of the vintners dazed with love among their vines is a telling image, but by no means an explanation. We want to have great wine explained. But what about ordinary *good* wine? If there's anything to this notion that a vineyard responds to being known and appreciated, is that response always in the form of the marvelous?

I'm thinking again of Erich Berger, whom we met in chapter 4. An importer like me is always aware of his competitors, both in his own areas of focus and across the entire world of wine. My Rieslings compete against the other guy's, and Riesling itself competes against other grape varieties for a claim on the drinker's attention. Competition makes us insecure. We hate to admit it because we have to exude confidence to make the sale, but we're always scared the other guy's wine will kick sand in our faces. So we fuss and strain to have *stellar* wines.

But there are types of wines that confound this assumption. Berger doesn't set out to make the "best" or highest-scoring wine; he wants to make *tasty* wine. "It was always drummed into me by the family, to be above all honest, straightforward, and willing to develop," he says. "It's why I want to make consistently good wines. I want my children to inherit values as I did as a child. My own philosophy is to always be in accord with nature and to understand the environmental signals it gives." Well, sure, you say; that's the usual boilerplate. But what I see is a thoughtful life of hard work in the service of wines that won't make him famous. He could force them to be more ostentatious. Every grower knows how, and Erich's land can give "impressive" wine. But he seems content to make self-effacing, enjoyable, and delightful wine, almost as if doing so were inextricable from his duties as citizen, father, and husband.

Willi Bründlmayer, one of the great Austrian vintners, said, "I try to get each vintage into a spirit close to *This is my first vintage* or *This is my last vintage*, in order to draw as much joy and affection for the grapes as possible. Chase away all routine and find the singularity of each vintage and of each grape."

Austria's Heidi Schröck puts it like this: "My inspiration is the vine itself. With its powerful roots it collects the life force which comes from deep below the surface. As the root system grows deeper and more complex, the wine becomes more interesting and multifaceted. Being in the vineyard helps me to understand nature and to know my own boundaries." Interesting, isn't it: a crux of viticultural experience is *something that you can't see*, something welling up from inside the world.

Sometimes a grower's inspiration is elusive. He probably couldn't put it into words. Sometimes it is so intimate he prefers to keep it to himself. At times he may not even know. I do not suppose this matter of inspiration is always linear—"I sing when I'm spraying because my dad always sang when he sprayed," or "I use yeast number 817-B because that's the one my dad used." When I first got to know Laurent Champs of the Champagne estate Vilmart & Cie., I saw a number of stained glass panels throughout the winery and cellars. Was it merely a leitmotif?

"No, actually," said Laurent. "My father is a worker in stained glass. You'll meet him when we go there for lunch."

Laurent's parents live in a timbered house in a woodsy dell. My knowledge of French is that of a moderately gifted kindergartner whose hobby is wine, but I managed to convey how much I'd enjoyed the stained glass. I was offered a peek into the workroom. It was as chaotic as most workrooms, a jumbly refuge with a boom box. What sort of music does a worker in stained glass listen to? I stole a glance at a pile of CDs, expecting to see Arvo Pärt or Hildegarde of Bingen, but all I could see was Miles Davis's *Kind of Blue.*

That first visit was twelve years ago. This year I asked Laurent how his father was doing. "He's working on a book," he replied. "The subject is the three Oriental religions, as seen through the symbolism of light, and what light means to them."

"Your dad's quite the mystic, isn't he?" I said.

"Oh, yes, very much so."

Laurent himself is capable and dashing. He's the kind of guy you imagine striding purposefully to catch his plane, wheeling very sleek luggage behind him. I've only seen a couple photos of him in jeans in the vineyards. But sometimes a veil will part, and he'll say something remarkable and searching. He once mused that 1996 "isn't a vintage of pleasure; it's a vintage of desire." I loved the deliberate ambiguity of that statement. It's wise in some way, to understand that desire is deeper than pleasure.

I sat with him in the cellar and thought about his father's book, a study in the mysticism of light written by a lifelong worker in stained glass, stories told in light, a narrative of the divine itself rendered by the divine. And Laurent is his father's son; his wines also express light, as if their flavors were swinging from a Jacob's ladder of luminosity. I had always seen Vilmart's Champagnes as infinitely yet tenderly bright—he uses a majority of Chardonnay in a commune where Pinot Noir typically rules—and now I wondered at the connection. Vilmart's best Champagnes are serene and *beautiful*. They are objectively wonderful and superb, like many wines I drink, but the others don't all move me as Vilmart's do. I scribbled in my notebook, and this is what I wrote: "Flavors as shafts of brightness, the eerie sweet feeling of being visited by whoever or whatever your god is, gods are; just that reassurance that we aren't forgotten, and that every tiny floating speck of dust is also deserving of the light."

I thought of asking Laurent, "Can you tell me exactly how your father's work influences your wines?" But it seemed rude and intrusive, and I wondered whether it was even necessary. I can *taste* the answer. And even if this is all a conceit of my imagination, the wines of this father's son compel such imaginings. I prefer to believe in these connections because the belief aligns with my intuitive life. In any case, it's harmless. It would be illuminating to hear why those who adamantly *disbelieve* in such connections—and for some reason it is always "adamantly"—feel the way they do.

Sometimes when I talk with growers they like to remind me that they're *farmers* first, before anything else. That's easy to forget if you're dealing with the New World, but in the Old—or the parts of it with which I'm involved—you never forget. Yet their world is not only farming; it's also selling, marketing, publicizing, engineering, and craftsmanship. If you plant carrots, you eventually harvest carrots. There are things you can do to ensure you have wonderful carrots, but once you put them in the customer's basket, your work is done. Imagine if picking the carrots were followed by processing them into a soup or a beverage that was then evaluated alongside everyone else's carrot product, deconstructed, given scores, and all of this so you can be ranked as a producer of carrot drinks. I don't know about you, but this would make me bonkers. Small wonder the vintner likes to be out in the vineyard where he can escape the noise for a while.

Knowing vintners helps you understand about palate, because you see how they steer their wines toward their own palate's preferences. I doubt if vintners ever construct an a priori *idea* of their wines—"I want to make a rugged, rustic wine with high alcohol"—rather, they make the kind of wine they themselves like. Later on they may describe their principles, but any overriding philosophy has arisen from their spontaneous preferences. As these develop, their wines change. Heidi Schröck started out making somewhat rural, antique-style wines, gentle, evocative, influenced by the acacia casks she had in the cellar. Later she began to favor more compact and focused wines, steering toward the brilliance she was learning to treasure.

She is not alone, but Heidi is one of the better tasters and more thoughtful folks out there. A common mistake among wine lovers is to assume that all growers have what we'd call good palates. Many do, but not all. The Germans have a tidy word, *Betriebsblind*, which describes the blindness (or lack of perspective) caused by overimmersion in one's own business. And yet even this isn't always bad. To be so imbued with the place and grape you work with that it is *inside you*, you are not separate from it, expresses such a powerful locating of identity in your wine that we drinkers experience it as soul. Such a pure unity of worker and place conveys a startling power. I remember hearing Ürzig's Alfred Merkelbach being asked if he ever took a vacation. Sigrid Selbach had been showing him pictures from a recent trip to South Africa, and he was clearly quite amazed. So where did he like to go?

He hemmed a little (as he often does when asked a direct question), and finally said, "Vacations? I don't really take vacations." Really? we asked him. With all the marvelous places in the world to see? "Oh, I don't know . . . where would I go? When I'm in the vineyards on a nice summer day, with the Mosel behind me, I have everything I need to be happy."

It is one thing to try to "understand" wine in terms of causes and effects by using the work of vintners grand and wonderful. Because the wines are superb we assume the story of their making to be significant. Sometimes it is, but that can never be the whole truth. The lives of Rolf and Alfred Merkelbach offer another angle for viewing an equally valuable *tranche* of truth.

No one knew who they were, except for a few merchants who bought wine in bulk from them and a handful of Mosel insiders. Luckily, one of those insiders was a friend of mine, the endearing Willi Schaefer, of Graach, with whom I'd made friends during my ten years living in Germany. I reached out to him immediately when I looked for estates to include in my first portfolio. We were happy to be back in touch, and Willi asked me whom I was considering working with. "Well, I was kind of hoping you could help me with that," I replied. "Who do you know who makes excellent wine that no one knows about?" He'd have to think that one over. And a day later he called, saying,

"Terry, I think you'll be happy at Alfred Merkelbach in Ürzig. Especially as you like my wines."

Off I went. I didn't make an appointment, and I went alone. I met two middle-aged Moselaners who looked as if they'd been sent by Central Casting to answer a request for colorful Old World German winegrowers. I think they'd never met an American. They were very shy, and answered many questions with a giggle. And they were very much a *they*, Rolf-and-Alfred. Their current vintage was almost sold out, but I'd be back next year to taste the new one from cask, before it was bottled or otherwise claimed.

In the early '80s there was nothing so remarkable about the Merkelbachs. They were small-scale (barely five acres of vineyards), hands-on, and obscure, in common with thousands of other Mosel growers in small villages. But two things were remarkable: first, it was just the two of them, for neither had married; and second, their wines were remarkable. And so we began doing business.

Over the years many things changed along the Mosel. Many of the small growers couldn't survive; they had no children who wanted to carry on, or they were part of the herd-thinning that occurred as wine scaled up from being an everyday part of life to being the purview of connoisseurs and "experts." An activist wine press came into being, and you had to make the cut if you were going to be successful. All the articles described the change in wine consumption, and the shorthand was, "We're drinking less wine but *better* wine." The old generation, who drank wine as a daily beverage without our fanatical concern for how "good" it might be, was dying out. And so the ordinary grower sold his vineyards, if he could, and folded up shop. If he had a child who wanted to continue, the young person knew the only way to prosper was to go all out for top quality and get on the journalists' radar. This meant lower yields (or so it was believed) and other investments, which in turn meant higher prices. Thus advanced the world, except for a small corner of it on the Brunnenstrasse in Ürzig, where Rolf and Alfred Merkelbach just carried on.

I arrived there one year to see a shiny white Volkswagen Jetta parked in front of the house. When Rolf and Alfred answered the door, I said something like, "Hey, some wheels, eh!" To which they answered, giggling, "Well, you bought it for us!" And I realized that the effect of my patronage was to keep this estate alive in its original form. It hasn't grown larger, and the prices barely seem to have budged, and these days people talk of Merkelbachs as if they were some open-air anthropological exhibit.

The brothers are adorable. They're older and more rumpled now, but everyone who meets them adores them. I have known them a quarter-century, and they remain as shy as the day we first met. That's probably why they remained bachelors, although the scowling-with-disapproval portrait of Mama in the parlor-cum-tasting room offers perhaps another clue. And I myself made hay from their cuteness in my writings for customers. But I got older, and something happened.

I say I've "known" Rolf and Alfred for all these years, but "known" isn't really apt. When I'm there we taste the wine and I enthuse and they giggle, and unless a Selbach is present (they act as brokers for me and often join my visits) there's hardly any schmoozing—sometimes even then. I'm sure the Merkelbachs are glad of me, but I have no idea what they make of me—nor I of them, if I'm entirely candid. Of course, I adore them, because they're adorable. But when I think of them now, I find myself immersed in a kind of mystery. Who are they? *What are their lives?*

They're closing in on age seventy now, yet they still do all the work themselves (with a little help at harvest), and the steep slopes are not for parvenus. They live simply and give every appearance of perfect contentment, and I believe they are contented. I *hope* they are; it's part of a faith I hold. Theirs are lives reduced to a degree of simplicity and integration we wouldn't tolerate. Now when I look at their adorable faces I hear an inner voice that both stirs and challenges me. *Look at those faces, and now tell me how valuable all your hip, arch postmodern affects are.* But not only that. *Feel the divinity in these simple lives.* I think of Zen, and how arcane and mysterious it all seems. Monks, retreats, silence, monasteries, all that jazz, and that strange calm no one seems to be able to explain. And here are Rolf and Alfred, effortlessly embodying the Buddhist ideal of contentment. They are at home in their lives. They have what they need to be happy. And they *are* happy. I don't know what they say to each other over breakfast, or in the vineyards, or how they decide what to watch on TV in the evening, and I have no idea what each man thinks as he's falling asleep at night. But I know they're happy.

And the mystery haunts the wines, precisely because the wines are anything but mysterious. Instead they're so *essential*, so euphorically pure and expressive they display a categorical identity you might be tempted to call honesty, except that "honesty" implies the option of being dishonest. Everyone who knows Mosel Riesling agrees; Merkelbach's wines are *ur*-Mosel, stripped of all affect or the artifices of ego. It's as if some kindly old Mosel-god speaks through these two shy men. And no one would claim the wines are "great," but to paraphrase Andrew Jefford, they are infinitely *good*. That this species of wine exists at all is great enough.

This hadn't occurred to Germany's Channel Two television when a producer sent out a reporter to film a brief "lifestyle" piece on the Merkelbachs. Alfred asked, with exquisite shy pride, if I'd like to see the DVD, and of course I would. The interviewer milked the human-interest angle, of course. Poor thing; it was rainy the day they shot, and she looked pretty forlorn in her slicker. Rolf and Alfred couldn't help being "colorful." If they were bemused at being described as the last of a dying breed, they didn't let it show.

The reporter got some footage of the housekeeper. She'd worked for the Merkelbachs for twenty-five years but would soon leave; her husband was ill and needed her full-time care. She was a stern-looking lady, the kind who weeps easily. Had she liked working for Rolf and Alfred? "Yes, it was good here," she said, as they quick-cut to the brothers at their little dinner table eating the meal she'd cooked. It was a ceiling shot that made them look very lonely. Who will cook for them now? Or maybe it was I who was lonely. I sat with my back to the room and cried, and hoped nobody could see me.

We left and walked to the other side of the village to our next appointment. My old friend Sigrid Selbach walked with me. I was still weepy. Sigrid put her arm through mine. I told her, "I haven't always been as good as I wanted to be, and there are things in my life I am ashamed of . . . *(pause)* . . . and at times I feel the weight of those regrets . . . *(pause)* . . . but something with which I can console myself is that I brought appreciation and prosperity to Rolf and Alfred during these years of their lives. . . . *(pause)* . . . I sometimes think of that." Sigrid, perfect friend that she is, looked into my face and said nothing.

eight

WINES THAT MATTERED
Or, "The Dog Ate My Point Scores"

This thing we tell of can never be found by seeking, yet only seekers find it.
—Abu Yazid al-Bistami

When you're new to wines, they all matter. You write
notes to focus your palate, hone your concentration, and
remember what you tasted. You read other people's notes, too,
so as to taste vicariously (especially if you can't afford the glam
wines you read about) and try to suss what tasting notes are
"supposed" to be, and whether yours measure up.

But eventually you reach a dead end with the whole tasting-
note thing. It becomes a form of absurdity. Most tasting notes
are associative (describing wine flavors in terms of other flavors), and this is of course tautological: saying a wine smells like
peaches is to say that peaches smell like peaches. Nor is it any
help if your reader has never smelled a peach.

There are basically two ways to taste wine. You don't have
to pick just one, but eventually most of us settle on the one that
comes naturally. You can taste "aggressively," that is, aim a beam

of concentrated attention directly at the wine, using your palate to take a sort of snapshot. This is entirely desirable, but taken to extremes it has the effect of seeming to torture a confession from the poor wine.

Or you can taste "passively," or peripherally; you look away from the flavors and see what the wine says when you're not trying to nail the sucker down. You quietly let the wine come to you. This approach brings you closer to the gestalt—I might even say the *truth*—of the wine. But the liability is that it's very hard to verbalize, unless your tasting note takes the form of a Zen koan.

On the other hand, for most of us, no one is going to read our tasting notes, so we can write whatever we want. I say this notwithstanding the distressing phenomenon of Internet wine bulletin boards wherein people share their tasting notes with other lonely wine geeks. I'm sure this is fun for them, but I find it a little sad. I have a melancholy feeling that lots of people spend their weekends drinking wine *in order* to post their notes on Monday. "Look what I drank!" The cork is pulled, and suddenly there are all these hypothetical eyes upon you. Your life becomes a kind of performance. But don't mind me. I'm just a private, introverted guy, and my relationship with wine has always been intimate.

As a merchant I have made myself write tasting notes because I want to help my customers determine what to buy, and because I seem to have lost the omniscient recall I had in my thirties, when I could remember every wine I tasted. These days I have to consult notes for a wine I tasted ten days ago. The job requires me to write notes on a thousand to fifteen hundred wines per year, which may be why I almost never write tasting notes at home.

But some wines embody a story—not merely a narrative, but a kind of curiosity, as if they cast out tentacles into the ether. Other wines stimulate the imagination, and you're off and running. I am very sure these things are worth getting down, but if you seek to share them you will sometimes run afoul of a certain kind of person who actually *does* want to know that your 2004 Domaine de la Crachoir tasted like "beer-battered kiwi fritters, boysenberries, and pork snouts." When Hugh Johnson's charming memoir *A Life Uncorked* was published, someone on the Internet was bemused. The book was useless to this person because "He never says how the wine tastes; he only says what it was like to drink it." Well, my good man, that there's the very *point* of the thing. I'd far rather read the genial musings of a humane spirit mulling over the little nimbus between his soul and the wine in the glass than to see how many arcane adjectives some anal geek can string together.

You've read such notes, I'm sure. *This dramatic wine has the burnish of torched sienna, that hint of Tuscan chickens, perhaps even pullets, that gamey, feathery aroma; a dishy first impression of guppies spawning and bracken roasting in the Castilian sun, and the high wind blowing from offshore when a garbage scow has recently run aground, not exactly fresh passion fruit, but passion fruit after it has been chewed by a horse that's just run through a heathery dale, you know, sort of sopping wet fetlocks and old dogs; and the finish, oh, just a portrait of nasturtium, or shuttlecocks dipped in quince jelly, or the stench on a fox's muzzle after he's eaten a number of small rodents or the ice caked in a refrigerator in a Paris apartment, or like new sandals, especially if the feet in them have been soaked in a bromide solution— and revisiting the nose is all rotty mulch sluicing out of a bilge pipe in a fetid stream of sweetly blooming hawthorn in a flighty perfume of freshly starched uniforms of a flight attendant in the first-class cabin in a manly swill of gassy medicinal opaline mordant porcine gratuitous acetate begonia-laden air freshener or like the fannings from a fire of souchong tea or like* . . . Somebody make him stop! *Just one more thing: Am I the only one who finds this wine a bit* hirsute?

One of the early wine books I read was the (tragically out-of-print) *Fireside Book of Wine*, a compilation done by the late Alexis Bespaloff. Among the works were many old tasting essays (it's mingy to call them mere "notes") by a few of the old-school British writers such as Maurice Healy and the great André Simon. If you read some of the travel literature of the nineteenth century, you'll discover that the ostensibly staid and prosaic British were wont to spout extravagantly emotional and flowery prose. As a fledgling reader of wine lit, I was getting the message that intense emotion was a normal response to intense beauty. I was in effect given permission to respond in this way myself. I was also reading Hugh Johnson, of course, and Gerald Asher's elegant columns in *Gourmet* magazine, and so all of the writers whose work shaped mine were either excellent writers or wore their hearts on their sleeves. People new to wine these days are just as apt to be corrupted as to be inspired; there's a lot of lousy prose and shallow thinking out there.

I want any tasting notes I care to read—my own or others'—to be *visceral*. Most of the time the telling image is more valuable than the literal description. You risk incoherence and self-indulgence if you write intuitively, and I'm sure I resemble that remark now and again, but it's a risk worth taking.

For laughs, I'll deconstruct a tasting note I wrote for a young wine while on the job. I was tasting at Müller-Catoir, a supernal estate in the Pfalz in Germany, and we were partway through the Rieslings. The wines were incandescent, as usual, and I noticed the way that beauty consolidates when you taste one superb wine after another. Each wine falls like a small snowflake, but they settle into a blanket of snow. We tasted a Spätlese from the Bürgergarten vineyard, and I wrote, "Well well well . . . so this is the view from the summit [I was still trying hard to be matter-of-fact] . . . Inconceivably exquisite. Plum essence in a perfect duck consommé. Spice spice spice. Mineral sings, 'Honey, I'm home!'" The wine was great, but I was essentially in control, lambent and receptive.

There was another Bürgergarten Spätlese, a sister cask to be bottled separately (reason alone to cherish German wines, this lovely determination not to sacrifice individuality). I thought we were through with the Spätleses. I wrote, "I didn't know this was coming. How do you get higher than the summit? Stand on tiptoes? Now comes the saltiness to shimmy into the sweetness and glide in an itchy, urgent gorgeousness over the palate [here it is, the precise moment I lost it and let myself be carried away] . . . profound and magnificent yet without opacity, rather delineated to the last molecule of detail." I tasted it again and again as if to break the spell, but the wine was bigger than I was, and I vanished through the membrane. "It tastes this way for the same reason blossoms open—for the bees to be useful, for the plant to live and make new plants, for a few human passersby to pause, sniff, delight, and feel a strange longing, not quite sad, wanting to touch another warm skin, oddly happy and alone in the odd lonely world."

On the surface the passage makes no sense. Yet it describes as accurately as my talents allow just how it was to taste that wine by saying where it took me. But first you have to surrender control, and then you have to be willing to risk looking silly. And it never works to force it. You let yourself dance to the particular music of that wine—which recalls a quote I like, from George Carlin: "Those who dance are considered insane by those who can't hear the music."

On the occasion when I wrote that note, I had a young colleague with me at Catoir. She didn't speak any German and couldn't follow the chatter, and I was loath to break the flow by pausing to translate. So she attended to the wines. At one point near the end, she rose and walked over to the oriel window, looking out into the gray March light. I knew why. She came back with glassy eyes and an out-of-body expression. Later in the car, as we headed to dinner, I said, "It's surprising how *wrenching* it is, don't you think?"

"Yes. Yes!" she said. "I mean, two or three of them you can withstand. But one after another, it just overtakes you."

For me, part of the fascination in how we respond to beauty is the very curiosity beauty engenders. *What is the nature of this experience?* I'll try to say how it is for me.

Beauty dilates the senses. That's the first thing that happens. Any beauty, whether of language, flavor, or sound. It penetrates us, and we absorb it with such a charged vividness that we suddenly grow aware of this quality's absence from ordinary experience. If the beauty is complex, we feel our minds scrambling to take it all in before it's gone, to make sense of it. This often happened for me at Müller-Catoir, and I was always constrained from examining it by the ambient conversation. They should have sat me in a quiet chapel and had a young novice monk bring me another wine every twenty minutes.

As the senses dilate to admit this strangely stunning beauty, a silence enters, too. For now, there is only *this*. You'd forgotten the mere world could include *this*, and something dormant in you awakens. The ordinary you will not suffice for *this*. Such beauty is a pledge to which you must attend.

As the senses focus and deepen and probe, the emotions also begin to dilate, unless you are inured or cold to beauty. The first things felt are gratitude and wonder. But there's more. Beauty is a fierce thing. It doesn't let up, it invades you, even *violates* you; it will have its way, and that way is ecstasy. And of the many notes in the ecstatic chord, one of them is rage. I don't know why, but it's there. Maybe it's because we can never seem to rise high enough to meet beauty at *its* level. Maybe it's because we spend so much time subduing rage and frustration, that when pure emotion is finally unleashed we get the whole sloppy mess, not just the pretty parts. Maybe the charge isn't selective—it electrifies all of you. The effect is strangely violent, even as it overwhelms you with pleasure.

And on the far side of this incandescence, we start to think of the people whose work brought this about. Suddenly their dedication seems astonishing. What does it entail, to offer this beauty? Sitting there receiving it, we suddenly grow somber. We're not thankful enough. Not just in this moment—*ever*. Yet we were invited.

And so we walk to the window with our back to the room, and weep.

In many cases the quietest beauty and the deepest stories live in older wines. That is in part because they grow less brash and frisky, less explicit—but more searching and, at best, more sublime. I have young colleagues who sometimes travel with me on my rounds in Europe, and I always thrill to see them respond to very old wines—in some cases older than they themselves are—for the first time. If you've never visited German growers you have no idea how these wines truly age, when they've never been moved from the perfect cellars where they've rested since the beginning. That first taste is nearly unbelievable, even if the wine is an unremarkable citizen of an ordinary vintage. There is a kind of *tenderness* in such wines, and many a grower, witnessing our wondering responses, has disappeared into his cellar to unearth another bottle, or bottles.

For many of these mature Rieslings it isn't just how well they've preserved, and it isn't even how many facets they've integrated or what complexities they've attained. It's more. It is, first, the extent to which they have stayed *alive*. They are neither relics nor objects of curiosity nor even of astonishment; they are still with us to serve their original purpose, to keep our food company and to make us happy. And it's also the way they've made peace among their factions of flavor. The French call this process *fondue*, a melting together of elements into a seamless whole. The tenderness I speak of arises here.

But it is also a quality of deliberateness. "A twenty-five-year-old Kabinett, and yet it tastes so *young!*" is not where it ends, but where it begins. The wine is going nowhere fast. It has much life before it, it has all the time in the world. Such wines do not only exist in time; they appear to *embody* it. We think of time as a thing there's always too little of, against whose relentless limitations we constantly bang our heads. But wine can show us another kind of time, a more meandering and forgiving time. There's an old saying: "The oxen are slow, but the earth is patient." Wine can bring us to the patient earth, of whose existence we are often not aware, though we live here. We do well to consider not only how wines age, but *why* they age. It is because they have something to show us, stories to tell us.

You could well be thinking, *Something to show us? What, exactly?* And if that were your thought, I would sympathize. I'd like to be more concrete, but the experience itself is too fluid. Still, I can offer an example. This evening I happen to be drinking a 1985 Riesling Grand Cru Kirchberg, from Louis Sipp (great name for a winery!) in Ribeauvillé, Alsace. The wine is almost a quarter-century old, and the bottle—luckily—is in excellent shape. It has the sort of *strict* character of Ribeauvillé Rieslings. It isn't hedonistic. But it begins with an up-close miasma of quince and ginger and a subtle stoniness. After an hour or so it gets a little crazy, like some potion of wild mountain herbs, Chartreuse almost, and tart berries like juniper. It's as if the wine were releasing something, its id, maybe. And after two hours, with the final bit in my glass, it's all burning leaf and kiln, but the oddest thing is how the flavor both compounds and retreats, on one hand growing ever more complex, and on the other drawing ever farther away. That sense of something wafting to you from across the hills and fields is awfully haunting. Maybe you've tasted it, and walked away, but my own weird temperament compels me to consider the spell. How many things bring it? How often? Why does it come, and what does it want? I find myself swimming in a liquid ether of leaves, trees, winds, burning. The leaves are burning because soon it will be winter. The trees will hunker down. They'll be bare and thready. We will see nature when it isn't putting on a show for us. Winter is like a dress rehearsal for death, but it isn't really death. It's just how we dip our toes in the dark water, and then go back to life. A long way to travel from a bottle of wine, isn't it? Yet really not very long at all.

Here's a wine with a story. During the decade I lived in Europe, from 1973 to 1983, I became solely and passionately devoted to wine. I promptly became a wine tourist, and one of the first places I visited right away was Burgundy. I lived in Munich, and Burgundy was closer than, say, Bordeaux, plus it was far more interesting and hospitable.

While there, knocking around earnestly (albeit cluelessly), I stumbled across a domaine off the main routes, in a corner of Beaune. I'll take a small degree of credit; even as a beginner I knew the wines were special. I bought what I could afford.

I returned a few years later. No appointment. Arrived just as a busload of Belgians was pulling away. The proprietor was doddering through the room consolidating the remains of tasting glasses into a large plastic bucket. "Ah, he'll top up his casks with that," I assumed. When all the glasses were emptied, our vigneron placed the bucket on the floor and issued a shrill whistle, whereupon his *dog* trotted in and proceeded to lap up what must have been several hundred dollars' worth of premier cru Burgundy. (Somehow I can't quite imagine a similar thing taking place in Pauillac. . . .) This time I had more money and I'd learned to allocate a lot of my Burgundy budget to this domaine, and so I bought and bought and bought.

And finally the very last of those bottles was being drunk, on New Year's Eve 2006. I had shipped it back from Europe along with its companions.

The bottle didn't look promising. There were at least three inches of ullage and, let's face it, I hadn't stored it perfectly. But these wines appeared indestructible, and a couple of months previously another old bottle from the domaine had been wonderful. So once more into the breach. Wine lovers all know the feeling—the final bottle! You can't stand to part with it, and in a strange way you almost want to wait till it's past its best; perversely, it's less heartbreaking that way.

The color was fine; mature, of course, but not decayed. It needed decanting to separate it from its heavy, gritty sediment, and even after the bottle had been vertical for forty-eight hours, the best I could do was leave an inch in the base. The bouquet of this wine was a force of spirit. If truffles had orgasms, they might emit this fragrance. Soy, sandalwood, shiitake, you know: Burgundy. Like the fat cap on a roast after you've studded it with cloves, sweet and caramelized and bloody. You know: Burgundy!

On the palate the tannin was durable and unpolished, in the old-fashioned way. Honest, nothing to be ashamed of. The fruit, or its echo, was something that reminded us how we blow silly things out of proportion. I could try to say what it tasted like, groping for literalisms, but I'd rather say it made me want to forgive. It melted away the trivial grudges I've clung to. It even said, Next year will be better, next year you'll let it go and let the kindness come.

We carved our roast, and my sweetheart and I sat down to dinner. The wine smelled like all the sweetness of the country, like the redeeming kindness of people. Thank you, old Albert Morot, for this Beaune Bressandes, 1969.

I love the varieties of beauty wine can display. Old Burgundy with its murmuring sensual depths, all the way to my cherished Riesling and its lyric, sprightly music. I am sometimes asked why I spend my career selling German wines. Did I see a marketing opportunity because the wines were so "underrated," or do I simply have freaky taste? I have, as you've noticed, a special fondness for German Rieslings along with a huge, unseemly crush on the entirely kinky Scheurebe, and drinking these wines, with their extraordinary vividness and complexity and delicacy, spoils one for wines of coarser virtues—which basically means everything that isn't German.

But for me it has become something other than the tastes of the wines *as such*. I glean a sort of meta-identity, a *species* of wine toward which I've become very fond.

One night while on my Germany rounds, I returned to my hotel, turned off the car, and climbed out into the early spring cold. And I heard a thing I hadn't heard in years: three nightingales were singing their dark and eerily beautiful song. Suddenly the world went silent and it was the beginning of time. I walked in the hotel's garden and listened to the three tiny birds until it was too cold to stay out any longer. Inside, I opened my windows—they were still singing there in the middle of the night—and snuggled under the comforter and let them sing me to sleep.

Each day as I'm making the case for German wines, I remember that night, and I realize that I am unnecessary; *nature* makes the case for German wines constantly, with every lark, thrush, or nightingale, every snap and crunch of apple, every swooningly fragrant linden tree in blossom, everything that makes us pause when we are visited by the electric hum of the world. German Riesling is a small bird that sings in the darkness, a seemingly minute thing that can tingle your pores, and haunt you your entire life.

To complete this tale, I should mention telling Helmut

Dönnhoff of my night reverie. Dönnhoffs are often considered among the world's most sublime Rieslings, and people feel an almost religious awe when drinking them. But the man himself is down-to-earth. "You wouldn't think those birds were so pretty on a hot July night when you're sleeping with the windows open," he rebuked me. "I want to take a rifle to the little bastards." Way to bust up my moment, dude!

Last summer my wife put a hummingbird feeder on our balcony, and lo and behold, they came—three of them, to be exact. I named them Nate, Alice, and Zippy. Nate is gray and handsome, with a long neck and a comely head, and if Alyosha Karamazov were a hummingbird, he'd be Nate. Alice is smaller, and she has emerald tail feathers. More skittish than Nate, Alice hovers when she feeds, while Nate will perch there as if no one could hurt him. The littlest one, Zippy, comes and goes. She never stays long. She seems a little hyper.

Nate is my favorite, because he will pause between gulps of sugar water and just look around. Hummingbirds beat their wings more than fifty times per second; they are extraordinarily kinetic. But in repose Nate looks like a miniature dove, a small happy saint, peering around with the pleasure of the world and a full belly. I was moved to see this little life pause and muse so calmly, just a few feet away.

It is precisely this equipoise of energy and delicacy that I love most about German Riesling. No other wine is quite the same. As I've gotten older I seem to have excavated some kind of compassion for little beings. I feel it when I think of Mosel Rieslings, especially a Kabinett or Spätlese with 7 or 8 percent alcohol, so slight you think it might not really be there, beating its wings faster than your eye can absorb, singing and singing.

It's curious how often Riesling and birds are connected. On one suddenly warm March day we arrived at the Karlsmühle estate in the little Ruwer valley near Trier. It would have been cruel to sit indoors. So we tasted alfresco, the way young Ruwer Riesling *should* be tasted, it so embodies the spirit of springtime. It was just the second time in seventeen years we'd been outdoors for our annual March tasting of the new vintage.

Bugs were buzzing and green was greening and everything alive was squirming with energy and even proprietor Peter Geiben's news that snow was forecast for the following week couldn't dampen our spirits. After an hour or so we all heard a sound from the sky and looked up, but didn't see anything. A moment later Peter pointed skyward and said, "There it is." It was two large flocks of migrating cranes, several thousand feet aloft and very small, headed north to their summer home in Russia. The two flocks were trying to join, milling and billowing as if to form letters in the sky, crying to one another to establish a flying formation, their cries echoing through the air as if they were lonely or afraid. But they only told each other, *Follow me, follow me. I sense a wind. . . .*

Sigrid Selbach was with us, and I reminded her of the previous time we'd been here when it was warm enough to taste outside. We set a table in the quiet parking lot, and the sun was in my eyes, and when the first wine was poured I turned my head to the left and spat onto what I *thought* was the ground, but it was in fact the dog's *head*. Poor old Sam. Lying there enjoying the sun just like us when *splat*, some plug of viciously high-acid young Riesling lands on his innocent head. This year I spat into a little bucket. I ain't into traumatizing no dawgs.

The wine had just been poured when we heard the cranes. It

was a Kabinett from the Nies'chen vineyard, and when I looked down into the glass it reflected the earth green and the sky blue, and when I sniffed this fresh little infant, with the lonesome birds calling one another, a thing was tied together from what had been only threads before.

A wonderful chef named Elka Gilmore once said to me that she wanted flavors so alive that they would be like holding your hand just below a ripe peach on its branch and the peach swoons down without even a touch because it is *ready* to surrender. A great young Riesling gurgles to you with all the delight of a baby playing peekaboo. Yet a whole sky was reflected in the glass, and a chorus of migrating birds played their eerie blue music.

But German Riesling is more than the lyric Mosel face. There's also the giddy extravagant Pfalz face (or "Pface") and the reserved, stoic Rheingau face. I used to work with a tiny family estate called Riedel, in Hallgarten, where they made passionately old-fashioned wines from barely seven acres of vineyards. The longer I bought from them, the richer I discovered their story to be.

Christine Riedel was nearing eighty years old when we first met. I'd been dealing with her son, Wolfgang, and she stayed in the background where she assumed she belonged. But she was hardly a weak-willed being; these were simply Old World manners. Wolfgang lured her out one morning with the promise of a venerable vintage to taste.

The wine made her less shy. I learned she had been widowed quite young, and that not only her husband but three of her four brothers had been killed in the war. She ran not just the household (or what was left of it) but also the wine estate, on her own. The Rheingau of those times was a region dominated by a few royal wine estates with lordly names. The small estates had little chance, and this small estate, with a mere *woman* running the show, had even less hope of survival. No one had reckoned on the irascible will of Christine! Her wines, improbably, were superb, leading the administrator of the most exalted estate in the region to call her "the top cellarmaster in the Rheingau."

It seems there was once a tasting to honor the birthday of Count Matuschka-Greiffenclau, proprietor in those days of the famous Schloss Vollrads. Christine Riedel showed the then-young 1959 Beerenauslese, which attracted the notice of the birthday boy. Thinking, I am sure, that he was offering the most cordial remark from a blue blood to a commoner, he permitted himself to observe to Frau Riedel how remarkable it was that a wine of such quality could come from a small vintner. He probably expected an awed curtsy. But Christine's life had been building to this very moment. "You know, Count," she replied, "our vineyards are less than two kilometers from yours. Do you imagine we receive the same sunshine, or does God in His wisdom hang a curtain between your vines and ours?"

The old wine Wolfgang had brought from the cellar was in a very tall bottle of thick green glass. The cork was eased out deliberately, still intact. The wine was poured quietly. It was deep greeny-gold, astonishingly; whatever it was, all that chlorophyll was still there. Oh, a *great* bouquet, enthralling, complex, a cathedral of fragrance, like leaves or tapioca pudding or orchids. As I was trying to fathom what it could possibly be, Wolfgang could no longer hold it in. It was a *1937* Hallgartener Jungfer Spätlese (an unexceptional wine), fermented dry, as was the rule of the day.

"That was the year I was married," Christine said. I couldn't stop looking at her face and her youthful blue eyes, and her hands as they held the glass. What things those hands have known. What life has passed before those eyes—an entire human life. The wine was majestic, dignified, almost theologically mysterious, with a sagey high note on the back of the palate and a smoky fall-evening mood of burning leaves; it had power and verve, it was still vigorous! It was full of ivy and grain. It told of a time when people dressed for dinner in their own homes. The room fell silent as we all opened our hearts to this winged messenger of time.

The wine itself was lovely, about as profound as wine can be, but the *experience* of drinking it with the woman who helped make it more than sixty-one years ago, and her son, and my friends, was overwhelming. I felt as if I'd received the tablets on which were carved the answer to every human riddle, but it was written in a language I did not read. It is hard at such times to think of wine as an isolated, discrete *thing*. Wine flows like blood through these lives.

Eventually Wolfgang spent more time attending to his first loves, art history and medieval religious architecture. The wines slowly declined as he became less interested. He sold off some of his best vineyards. The little estate's clientele of private customers was aging and didn't buy much anymore. I was very fond of Wolfgang and wanted him to be happy, but I mourned another loss in a vanishing world, story upon story, flame upon flame snuffed out. My tribute is paltry against the passionate dignity of these lives.

At times the serving of old vintages is ceremonial, but not always. Sometimes it's almost casual, as among close friends with a shared interest. (It always surprises me when people are indifferent to old wines, or when they taste but don't "get" them.) One year while I was visiting my portfolio's Champagne growers, I had a young colleague along, and when we arrived at Gaston Chiquet in Dizy, Nicolas Chiquet wondered what his birth year was. A birth-year wine was still a rarity to my young chum, but Nicolas has lots of vintages in the cellar and so the boys went off to scrounge around underground.

I sat alone in the living room in a state of advanced bliss. I hadn't expected it. I'd been around people—congenial, even beloved people, but still—every day for the past two-plus weeks, and the sudden solitude was a balm I didn't know I needed. The blackbirds kept me such company as I required with their noisy melodies. It was just after sunset, and they sang as if they'd been caught unaware by the twilight. I had three of my favorite things at hand: solitude, songbirds, and Champagne.

Nicolas returned with a 1981 in tow, along with the '88 and '85 vintages of his top bottling (known as Special Club). We started with the '88, which had been the available vintage when I had first visited this estate twelve years earlier. Alas, like a fool I had drunk all my own bottles before they were really ready—I may be smart but I'm not patient—and I remembered again how the '88 took its sweet time maturing. This '88 Club was disgorged in 2007, and man, it was surreal, with haunting fruit and texture and a vein of chalky terroir to balance; fennely and mentholated and long; not powerful but incisive and remarkable; one of those *Well, this comes from somewhere* wines. Not a wave crashing against the rocks, but a full moon rising over dark fields. So we drank it and continued to the '85 and '81, relaxed and thoughtful, schmoozing accompanied by splendid old Champagne.

At times, though, it starts out innocuously enough, tasting an old vintage to honor another year of friendship and good business. But it can morph unexpectedly, and then it is very hard to be me, because the fugue state that ensues is a solitary one, and I'm shy about being über-emotional in a crowd.

I work with a Champagne grower named Geoffroy, and old wine has been a leitmotif for us since the beginning, when I surprised Jean-Baptiste Geoffroy (and believe me, myself) by correctly guessing four of the five vintages he poured me blind. "Are you some sort of *savant?*" he asked. Not a chance. It was easy, as I tried to explain, because the aromatic signatures of these Champagne vintages were very close to the same vintages in Germany, which I knew extremely well. So now, when our business is done, we taste something venerable, and one year Jean-Baptiste announced, "This year I'd like us to taste something in honor of my grandfather."

He disappeared into the cellar, returning with a wormy old bottle from what he said was his grandfather's time. The cork sighed out. The wine was poured, a serene, deep straw color. Oh, it was a perfect old-wine fragrance; mocha, carob, could almost be red Burgundy. The word *spellbinding* came to mind. A deep, tender old friendliness, sweet with history. Almost impossible to assimilate; it was berserk with intricacy.

Jean-Baptiste's father came in and joined us; he'd been busy in the cellar. "Started without me, I see!" he remonstrated.

The wine was a 1966. So juicy still, so redolent of burning leaves and winter truffles. What a vintage! A slightly scorched note came on as the fruit faded. Next Jean-Baptiste's wife, Karin, came in, carrying the new baby, with another daughter at her side. The older girl seemed about six. She took the baby, who looked around and cooed. Old wine, new life, what can you do? *It all floods in.*

How many "points" is *this* worth? Lives lived in wine; three generations sitting with us and paying tribute to a fourth. "When I taste a wine like this, and think of my grandfather's methods," said Jean-Baptiste, "why change them?"

In old wine, life is restored to us with all the bad stuff removed: no fights, no illnesses, no misery. Only the stately passing of seasons, again and again. Only the love, the strange indifferent love without *affection*, the love you hear between the notes and the sentiment.

Twenty minutes went by, and now the wine smelled celestial: scallops drizzled with butter and nutmeg, macadamias, spices, star fruit. The six-year-old was offered a taste. She tasted like a pro: sniffed, swirled, drew air into her small mouth. Did she like it? She was very shy around us strangers, but she managed to peep out a tiny answer: "Il est bon."

There is the reason to care about wine. There is the taproot. Each of the many times I've shared an old vintage with this family, there have been three generations present (and most recently a two-week-old rabbit named Noisette whom the youngest child wasn't letting out of her sight), and we taste without ceremony at the old table, and I watch as this particular form of beauty gestates within a family and a culture, an understanding that this is worth doing, that people can live good lives doing this.

In case you are thinking it's easy to be seduced by the romance of it all when you're over there with the family drinking their Champagne with the smells of lunch cooking, you're wrong. I am sentimental about many things, but not about beauty. Beauty is too important to be sentimental about, and besides, beauty is often hard and indifferent. The spell can steal over you at any time and in the most prosaic circumstances, unless you have made great efforts to insulate yourself against it. This I think is the key; to be available for the spell is very easy. All you need to do is calm down and look around. To be impervious to the spell requires a far greater effort—plus it costs more in lost quality of life. I suspect most of you would agree, in theoretical terms, but you're wary whether a mere wine can deliver such moments of meaning. We're terribly proud of being down-to-earth where wine is concerned. I know a guy who spends about ten times more than I do on wine and who'd pooh-pooh every word of this book. "Goes down, stays down" is his highest praise. The part of this take that's right is completely right; the only problem is, there's a vast part of it that he has refused to consider.

Yet I sympathize. The sacred without the profane is merely precious (just as the profane without the sacred is merely dirty), and there are loads of times when all you need to say is, "This is fucking great wine." I had a 2004 Muscat the other night from Müller-Catoir, and the *F*-word was flying around the room with every sip. It'd be fun to read a tasting note like, "Oh, man, fuck; I mean, not just fuck, but *FUCK*." I'd buy it, wouldn't you? In any case, it says more to me than the "melted licorice, road tar, and weasel dandruff" school of tasting notes.

The wine itself steers your response. A quiet, pensive wine won't propel you up from the sofa spewing profanities, unless that's, you know, your basic default position in life. One day last spring it had been stormy since early morning, rumbly and gloomy. Outside, the trees in Maryland were just leafing, in that virginal unbelievable green that's like no other. The leaves were still curled and modest, and from my eighteenth-story balcony the trees looked like a lace curtain of emerald. It was getting on toward dusk and the storms were passing, and a sudden moment of sunlight threw crepuscular rays against the black of the retreating sky as the rain blew north. For a few seconds the whole sky was a drama, a tragedy, a miracle that the hero didn't see.

I didn't plan it, but the wine in my glass was an obdurately youthful 1990 Riesling from my friends at Nikolaihof in Austria's Wachau. It was the Weingebirge Smaragd, all of 12.5 percent alcohol, and so pale and limpid I almost couldn't accept the ripe balsamic sweetness of the fragrance. I really don't know how this experience assumed the form of a "tasting note." I just know that when I stood with the glass on my balcony and looked at the sun-on-black of the vanishing storm and the sun-on-green of those wet new leaves, dark, light, and gleaming all at once, I knew there was no other wine that could possibly make this moment liquid.

Wines like these don't seek to be included in the world, or even in your world, because they already are. They didn't ask your permission, any more than the rain does or the leaves do. When you drink them, they *include* you. This is so unusual, this feeling of being invited and included, when so much of our experience is confined to being indulged or entertained.

Is there really enough time to waste on the unreal? But who am I to know what is real and what is false? Nobody; I have no authority. I only report what I experience. You're free to ignore me. But I know what I know, and there's no doubt in it. And I know that every time we accept the flashy in place of the true, we starve a being who lives inside us. A modest being, who won't even say when he is hungry—but late in your life you will see he is there, and there's no time left to know him, and he had so much to say to you.

E ven if I'm unusual in the degree to which I welcome the spell, it's hard to deny the uncanny ways wine embodies connections. Here is a story.

When I was in my early forties, I decided to search for my birth parents, having been adopted as an infant at a time when adoption was a very hush-hush matter. Eventually, and with the help of a detective who specialized in such things, I found them both, both alive, though no longer with each other (they were high school sweethearts), both in good health, and willing to see me.

It was biomom (as I came to refer to her) who led me to biodad. Biomom had been looking for me, and her suspicions were aroused by a phone call she'd gotten from the detective, whose ruse she didn't believe. So ours was a mutually welcome reunion. Biodad, on the other hand, had to be contacted out of the blue.

This man and his wife demonstrated new depths of human decency and kindness in the welcome that greeted my approach to them. But that's a tale for another time. Our first talk was over the phone, and I made haste to assure him I was a successful adult and professionally well-off—some who search are in straits—but in that first dazed conversation I didn't tell him exactly what it was I did for a living. We talked in a rearranged reality, and about ten minutes after signing off, he called me again. "I guess I'm not through with you yet," he said.

"So, give me a sense of you—what are your hobbies?" he asked.

"Well, I enjoy the mountains and love to hike, and I play the guitar and love music and have never quite abandoned my dream to be a rock star," I said. "And you?"

"Oh, you know, I'm a Jewish doctor, so I love to play golf." He chuckled. "And other than that, I suppose you could say I consider myself something of a wine aficionado."

"*Really?*" I said, trying gamely to pick up my jaw off the floor. "And are there any wines you particularly like, any favorites?"

"Well, I know they're not the most popular wines around, but I must admit I have a soft spot for German wines. . . . Hello? Are you still there?"

"Let me tell you what it is I do for a living," I stammered, and once I'd told him he said, "Wait a second, stay on the phone, I'll be right back. . . ." I heard his footsteps retreating and, in a moment, returning. "I have your wine in my cellar! My son gave me a case for Christmas last year."

And that is my wine story. Remember it the next time someone says you shouldn't take wine too seriously.

If wine connects to life, as I believe it does, then it connects to birth and to death. Old wines, especially, have a grave tenderness that consoles the darkness. I have often seen these old wines linked to the memory of the people who made them; you've heard the story of the Geoffroy tasting, and I can't forget a bottle of 1953 offered to me at Willi Schaefer to mark the twenty-fifth anniversary of our meeting. It was all of ten in the morning, but Willi's wife, Esther, was with us, and when the wine was opened she poured a glass and said, "Let me take a glass to your mother, Willi; she'll enjoy drinking a wine her husband made." I didn't know what part of the house was the widow's, and I'd never met her before, but it was exquisitely touching to think of her drinking this wine. What, really, was the fluid in that glass?

One year, as my "entourage" and I arrived at Stefan Justen's estate (on the Mosel again, but these growers seem to have the deepest collections of old vintages), I learned the melancholy news that his father had finally succumbed to the emphysema with which he'd struggled for many years. He was two weeks dead, but his son's demeanor was opaque (Moselaners are unfailingly correct except with intimates). But when he brought out the old wine, he told us it was in tribute to his father. Pause with me just a second. The wine was poured, and the glass lifted in condolence and sympathy and gratitude, not only for the wine itself, but for our inclusion inside the circle. At this moment, how it tasted doesn't matter. Wine makes life liquid and tangible. Father had died and we raised a glass to him, we who had known one another for many years and were united in the love of these wines, which brought us together at the start and had brought us together again.

Usually I sniff the wine for clues, but this was like nothing I'd ever encountered. The color was deep but not at all golden; rather, a chlorophyll-saturated thick green. The fragrance was sappy, verdant, boxwoody, forest floor. The palate was gorgeously confusing, full of old-wine mystery but still *stiff* and crazily fresh. It was dry—Stefan thought perhaps 30 grams per liter (3 percent) of sweetness; in those days a wine fermented until it felt like stopping. It was one of his final three bottles, he said, and he himself was tasting it for the first time. Were we ready to know what it was?

A *1945*, one of only three wines made by the Justens in that great tragic vintage. The wines were made by widows, grandparents, and children in the settling dust of the cataclysm. This wine was hidden from the occupying French until they withdrew in 1948. It was my first '45, too, and I was muted, flattened. There were wet eyes among my companions, but it was too sudden, too unreal for me; I needed this wine at the end of an evening of intimate conversation with beloved friends. We were late for our next appointment, and here was this strange green sap dancing in the glass as if it were immortal.

Although I'm very chummy with many of the growers with whom I work, Justen isn't one of them. We don't yuck it up. But each year he brings some old wines out when we've finished the work of tasting the new vintage. Stefan is a reserved sort of man; wine is how he conveys the value he places on our relationship. It is almost unbearably touching, and I can never let it show.

Still, emotion lives by its own rules and when it wants to appear there's little one can do to curtail it. Sigrid Selbach, as I've mentioned, sometimes joins me on my rounds among Mosel growers. One of her oldest friends is Hans-Leo Christoffel of the estate Joh. Jos. Christoffel in Ürzig, to whom I was introduced in 1986. Sigrid and Hans-Leo were school chums, and though each married other people—very happily in both cases—theirs is a rare chemistry, which takes the form of them cracking each other up. I am sure that in some way my holistic experience of tasting Christoffel is informed by their constant laughter.

One year when our work was done, Hans-Leo drolly asked if we wouldn't "mind" tasting something back a few years, having worked up quite a thirst tasting the new vintage. We supposed we could be persuaded.

The wine had that wonderful color in transit from young green to grown-up gold, a kind of palimpsest of youth and maturity. I figured it was between twenty-five and thirty years old—with that color it couldn't possibly be older. It had an entirely heavenly Mosel fragrance that grew smoky as it sat in the glass. The palate was long and dry, with delicate smoke in the finish; just lovely in its calm, meditative way. Guessing the vintage would be difficult, but I was pointing toward 1966. Wrong. The wine was a 1959, an Auslese, not one of the huge ones for which the vintage is famous, but a delicate one from the same parcel the current "three-star" hails from. I had never tasted such a youthful and pensive '59, and while I was wondering at its beauty I glanced over at Sigrid; she was chuckling with Hans-Leo, just as these two friends have done since the first time I'd seen them together twelve years earlier.

Sigrid first brought me to this house, and now here we were again, drinking this '59—the year Johannes, her eldest, was born. I started to cry because I didn't deserve to be there. I'd had too many hands in too many cookie jars in my life. Silly, isn't it? In order to try to *be* worthy, and because I felt so sentimental, I rather ceremoniously thanked Sigrid for bringing me here and for all the things that had led to this moment, trying desperately to keep my voice from breaking. "Oh, now; it's too early in the day for such compliments!" she sang out. And, perfectly, the moment dissolved.

It occurs to me that we all are acquainted with "spiritual" experience in various everyday forms. Think of nostalgia, a sudden awareness that time has passed, when our old life assumes a roseate glow and the life to come seems all too brief. I suspect that anyone who has ever signed divorce papers has had a moment of transcendence, no matter the relief. It has ended, the dream has ended, the hopes and the plans, and now that you're no longer fighting with this appalling Other you remember that you loved this person, and for many years you made a life and managed not to maim each other. And now you're just another person who failed, that's what it feels like, and suddenly you realize how *hard* it all is, trying to be half-decent and fair and loving and to live with your own disastrous personality, and we're all milling and colliding in the dark, and there is a great sorrow in it, but it somehow isn't exactly *sad*. My point is not that we should live in such a state all the time; it would kill us, not to mention bore those around us to catatonia. My point is that such states are a part of life, that wine can deliver them, and that it simply *makes no sense* to exclude them forcibly, as we far too often do.

If I live in a world with other beings who are as real as I am, I can never be entirely lonely. I can't make you feel this, though I can ask you to trust me. It isn't weird. Its *absence* is weird, and its deliberate absence when we ourselves have shoved it away is perverse. We're all afraid to die, but that's not nearly as sad as the number of us who are afraid to *live*.

Do I stretch my point too far, linking mere wine to questions of life and death? I'll entertain the thought. We are not all made the same way. We have to live the lives that come naturally.

I had a friend in Austria who was about the sweetest man who ever trod the earth but cast an indulgent eye toward my more mystical wanderings. The fiend would present supernal old vintages of his wines and then tease me when I sank into the spell they cast. Yet each year he brought another one out, and there I went into my silly trance. He'd cock his head as if to say, *You know, it is just wine*, and I'd cock my head back as if to say,

Well, in that case, why've you spent your whole life making it? Thus our affectionate impasse.

His name was Erich Salomon, and he was one of the many new people I met when I was first researching Austrian wine and assembling my portfolio. There were many remarkable personalities (the ebullient Ludwig Hiedler, the genial sage Willi Bründlmayer, the elegant-earthy queen Heidi Schröck . . .), but perhaps none as striking as Erich. There was a cheerful affection about him, as if he possessed a rogue gene that made him quiveringly ready to be delighted by the world. Happy the man who is born that way. It is entirely apart from the cultivation of optimism as a point of view. That never works. It is, rather, a piece of absurd good fortune to find in life a source of such cheer. In Erich it took the forms of generosity, collegiality toward other vintners, an instinct to kibitz, and affection for nature. I'll never forget his healing a tree that had been stabbed by the tines of a forklift. He bandaged the bark and watched over the wounded tree as if it were human. And a year later he showed it to me proudly and joyfully—"See? It's all better. You can hardly see the wound."

His wines, of course, were lovely, and imbued with his caring spirit. He didn't fuss over his sales. Each year he greeted my friends and me in his sweet, teasing way. And then one year he said he'd been ill. Didn't go into detail, but it would be like Erich to downplay it anyway, such was his tact. I didn't press; he'd tell me what he wanted me to know.

The following year brought the news that Erich's younger brother Bert would leave a career in wine marketing to assume control of the estate, with Erich at his side. Neither of Erich's two children was interested in being a vintner, and Bert's arrival was a perfect solution.

As the years passed, I'd see them together at times, and at other times I'd be told Erich was ailing but sent his greetings. One year he was in India on an ayurvedic cure. Last year when I visited the estate, I asked after Erich and was told he was on the mend from a debilitating flu that had laid him up for weeks, but that he'd be out to say hi. It was a mild spring day, and my group sat under the linden tree that Erich had nursed back to health all those years ago. Some of those traveling with me had never met him. I wondered how he'd be. And as we were an hour or so into the tasting, I heard a familiar voice, and there was Erich, loping across the courtyard with a huge grin and an entirely bald head. "It's my Bruce Willis phase!" he said. He looked hale enough, and he sat with us for ten minutes or so, saying little. He seemed almost apologetic, as if he didn't want to obtrude on our work on such a fine spring day. I tried to draw him out about India. I would have sat there forever talking with him. But he took his leave and strode back into the house, holding close the extent to which he'd had to rally his strength to come sit with us.

That was May. In December arrived the news I dreaded, that the cancer had killed him. He was in his mid-sixties but seemed younger. Men like Erich always seem younger. The evening we heard the news, my wife and I opened a bottle of a 1982 Riesling Erich had made, and which we had recently received. Karen had barely met Erich, but I needed to drink this wine with her.

The bottle was good, with a clean cork, a good, healthy color. Old wine does a trick, or something that seems like a trick. It starts out almost stale and musty, smelling not of itself but of the cellar in which it lay dormant and beating. In the first instant all old wines smell alike; they smell like "old wines." This one did, too. So we sat and drank this taciturn herald of time and memory and thought about the man who made it. Seven years before, Erich had renewed the lease on the vineyard from which it came, a site owned by the monks of the Abbey of Passau, who still receive a tithe of its production. He had told me the story of the ceremony when the new lease was signed, wondering who would be present for the next renewal, thirty years later.

The following spring when I was back at the estate, we sat with Bert and his family while a bottle of his and Erich's grandfather's wine, from the 1943 vintage, was served. At my request, we joined hands around the table. The wine seemed so fresh as to suggest the eternal. I thought of the '82 I had drunk that evening with my beloved. I remembered how it sat in our glasses, mute at first. And then suddenly, miraculously, it transformed itself, it found the fruit and tenderness with which it was born, it seemed to exhale in pure relief, free at last from the confines of the bottle, and the dark cellar. It sat there in our glasses, and my wife and I watched in wonder as it rose from the dead.

ACKNOWLEDGMENTS

I wish I had thought of this book's title all by myself. In fact, the man who thought of it was New York restaurateur Peter Hoffman, who hosted a wine dinner featuring a poetry reading between courses, and wines. Of course, I'd have thought of it eventually. Of course.

Robert "Bobby" Kacher got me my first job in the wine business. He took a leap of faith. I had no experience and was quite a wine bore. Although he and I disagree at times, and our philosophies could be said to be at odds, he is a great hero. He knows himself and is faithful to his truth—he has integrity.

Howard G. Goldberg first "discovered" me, in 1987, when my fledgling portfolio showed well in a tasting he attended. He has been an unfailingly generous and not entirely uncritical angel ever since.

David Schildknecht was in retail when we first met. We quickly became brothers in arms, and have remained so even as our interests have diverged.

Among the many people who have offered encouragement

and support beyond the call, Howard Silverman, Bill Mayer, Tom Schmeisser, Paul Provost, and Hiram Simon all stand out.

The first sommeliers to put my wines in their programs were real pioneers. They included Scott Carney, Andrea (then) Immer, Daniel Johnnes, and Steve Olsen. All are still in the industry in various capacities, and none has suffered an apparent neck injury from having stuck it out as far as they did.

Alice Feiring was instrumental in helping me find an agent and publisher. When I asked her we were barely even acquaintances, but she assisted me with a touching and nearly incredible generosity.

Marnie Old took time and care with this project, for which I thank her.

Betsy Amster is a wonderful agent and critic and friend.

Blake Edgar has been kind beyond measure as I taxed his patience with this manuscript.

I work with outstanding people. Kevin Pike, Liz DeCesare, Jonathan Schwarz, and Leif Sündstrom are all much more than colleagues; they are kin. My association with Michael and Harmon Skurnik has been a joy from the first moment, and remains the best move I ever made—in a rare moment of wisdom and lucidity—since entering the wine business.

Without the sage council and abiding friendship of Peter Schleimer, I could never have launched my Austrian wine program, not to mention I'd be a much less happy guy.

I thank every single vintner whom I have ever represented for the privilege of being associated with their fine work, and for the trust and friendship they have shown me.

But one family stands out. And a story wants to be told.

After I made my first trip to German wine regions, in May 1978, I returned in a state of fanatic wonder. And I immediately set about locating all of Munich's fine-wine retailers to see what I could buy close to home. One of these shops was in a basement in a near-in suburb, and I was browsing during my first visit when I heard the proprietor's voice admonishing a customer in tones of nearly theatrical snootiness. I looked around and caught sight of a young man, apparently an employee, with whom I exchanged a mutual raising of the brows.

I approached him and asked, "Did he really just say that to the guy?" and received the reply, "Oh, he's just warming up; it gets worse as the day goes on." And we were off and running, the first words of a friendship that is in its thirty-second year. I learned the young man was the son of a winegrower named Strub, in Nierstein, a village I had just visited. "Next time you come, please stop in at my winery," he invited.

Walter Strub was in the middle of his *Wanderjahr* when he had to return to the estate. His father had suffered a heart attack and his mother had burned her hands; Walter was needed. I visited him many times over the next four years, and we sat up many a night saving the world over bottles of wine at the kitchen table, as young men do. When I was preparing to return to the United States, Walter drove the four hours to Munich to pack up my cellar and have it shipped for me. He was the first vintner to let me taste prebottled wine before *dosage* was blended in to adjust the final sweetness.

When I conceived the notion of creating a German wine portfolio a few years later, Walter was the first person I visited. By then there was Margit, whom he soon married. I have worked with Strub's wines since day one, and have spent more pleasurable hours with him and Margit than with anyone else I know.

This might not have happened had I confessed an appalling transgression I perpetrated early on. It was July, and I was in Germany putting the first version of my portfolio together, and I started with a visit to Nierstein, where Walter and Margit put me up in their attic guest room. It was my first day, I was jetlagged, and we had stayed up far too late and drunk an absurd quantity of wine. Sometime in the night I had to piss with great ferocity. The house was dark, and its narrow wooden stairways were steep and creaky. I could turn on the lights and wake everyone, or try to stumble down and risk a serious and noisy fall. To make things worse it had started to rain. Hard. But that gave me a hideous idea. I could piss out the window! The rain would wash it away, and no one would ever know. Ahhhh-h-h-h!

When I rose the next morning I looked out my window and saw I had pissed on Walter's father's *car*, and when I confessed this sordid business many years later, to gales of laughter, Walter said, "My father could never understand where this green spot came from on his roof!"

When Hans Selbach died, I arranged to fly over for the funeral. I'd be on the ground less than thirty-six hours. I phoned Walter and said I'd drop by—Nierstein is twenty-five minutes from Frankfurt airport—to drink a pot of tea before making the two-hour drive to the Mosel. "Don't do that," Walter said. "I'll pick you up, and we can drive to the Mosel together, and then I'll bring you back to Nierstein." Hearing the friendship in his words, I nearly wept. He'd save me the expense, the exhausted drive, and the solitude. This is what a friend does.

Lifelong friendships will invariably fly through weather from time to time, as ours has, and might again. But there isn't a single day I am not grateful to the Strub family—Margit, Walter, Sebastian, Johannes, Juliane, even Emma the piddling beagle (like I'm one to talk . . .)—for the simple miracle of being such good people. This book is written with love for them all.

Designer: Nola Burger
Text: 10/15 Janson
Display: Bodoni Roman
Compositor: BookMatters, Berkeley
Printer and Binder: Maple-Vail Book Manufacturing Group